COMPOSITE DRAWING
Techniques for Architectural Design Presentation

COMPOSITE DRAWING
Techniques for Architectural Design Presentation

M. Saleh Uddin

McGraw-Hill
New York San Francisco Washington, D.C. Auckland Bogotá
Caracas Lisbon London Madrid Mexico City Milan
Montreal New Delhi San Juan Singapore
Sydney Tokyo Toronto

Library of Congress Cataloging-in-Publication Data

Uddin, M. Saleh (Mohammed Saleh)
    Composite drawing : techniques for architectural design
presentation / M. Saleh Uddin.
        p.   cm.
    ISBN 0-07-065749-1 (hardcover)
    1. Composite drawing—Technique.   2. Architecture—Designs and
plans—Presentation drawings.   I. Title.
NA2714.U33   1996
720′.28—dc20   96-20439
                                                CIP

McGraw-Hill

*A Division of The **McGraw·Hill** Companies*

1 2 3 4 5 6 7 8 9 0   IMP/IMP   9 0 1 0 9 8 7

ISBN 0-07-065749-1

*The sponsoring editor for this book was Wendy Lochner and the
production supervisor was Thomas G. Kowalczyk.*

Design, electronic layout and composition by M. Saleh Uddin.

Cover drawings:

Left drawing in color: Murphy/Jahn Architects

*Right drawing in black and white: Joseph Dreher, Student, Savannah
    College of Art and Design*

Back cover drawing: M. Saleh Uddin

Printed and bound by PrintVision.

Contents ■

ACKNOWLEDGMENTS

This book is dedicated to those architects and illustrators who generously participated in this project and took their time to explain their drawings via phone, fax, letter and overnight mail.

I would particularly like to extend my appreciation to the following people for their important contribution to this publication effort:

• Architects and illustrators from Japan, Australia, Malaysia, Korea and China for their quick response and respect for the project.
• Office of Murphy/Jahn, Kajima Corporation (Japan) for their prompt submission.
• Office of Bernard Tschumi and Scogin Elam & Bray for their last-minute contribution of reproductions.
• Bryan Cantley of Synesis, Steven House, Art Zendarski, Scott Howe (Japan) for their enthusiasm and trust in this project.
• The students in my design studio and graphic communication classes both at Southern University, Baton Rouge, Louisiana, and at The Savannah College of Art and Design, Savannah, Georgia, for their many contributions.
• George Loli (University of Southwestern Louisiana), Tom Sofranko (Louisiana State University) and Ron Yong (Houston) for their input in rearranging various chapters and editing images.
• Nan Blake (The University of Texas at Austin) for her help in editing portions of the text.
• Special gratitude is extended to my wife Mahmuda, daughter Shehreen and son Zaheen for their encouragement and support.

PREFACE

∎ The original intent and idea in preparing a book on Composite Drawing came from observing my students struggling for reference materials on a total presentation format in their design studios.

∎ There are a number of books on architectural graphics and rendering. Most deal either with beginning level of technical graphics or advanced rendering emphasizing perspective presentation. Also there are few books dealing with exotic but ambiguous images without having any clear explanation of their intent and interpretation. The primary goal of this book is to bridge the gap between those extremes and to explore some important devices used in a total design presentation of architectural ideas.

∎ The beginning of the book deals with techniques and conventions of architectural presentation drawing emphasizing exploration of drawing, media and technique. The next portion deals with composition and combining individual drawings into one image. The last half covers composite images from the professional arena. Each composite image is accompanied by the concept of the design along with an explanation of the drawing.

∎ It is my hope that this book will be a source of ideas not only for composition, technique and media, but more importantly, for initiating design concepts as well.

Mohammed Saleh Uddin
Baton Rouge, Louisiana

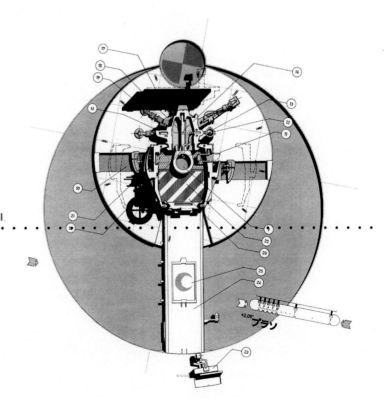

Outhouse Prototype by Bryan Cantley + Kevin O'Donnell.

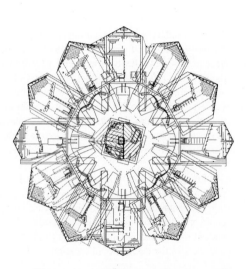

Introduction ■

INTRODUCTION

Attitudes and technical conventions in design presentation have not changed significantly in the past few hundred years. Even though drawing and rendering equipment and other tools have improved, we have not seen any new drawing types since the invention of perspective theory in the Fifteenth Century. (The theory of axonometric drawing or parallel projection, another convention of three-dimensional drawing, also dates back to the Italian Renaissance.) Compared to the invention of still photography and its elaboration into the motion picture, architectural drawing formats and conventions have lagged behind. Even the advent of electronic technology has led toward the refinement of presentation drawings rather than creating new types.

As long as the primary purpose of architectural drawings is construction, with aesthetics playing a peripheral role, architectural drawings are generally limited to technical information and are thought of as individual pieces, individual technical drawings. If a new approach could be achieved that would bring together all known conventions (plan, elevation, section and 3D views), architectural drawing would move into a new arena where the comprehensive overview of the design could be as important as its technological base.

Architects and designers have begun to experiment very recently with multi-media presentation techniques for architectural drawings. As experimentation progressed, drawings evolved into the hybrid expression of several drawings combined into one, creating interest within the general population as well as in the design community itself. In many instances these new architectural drawings, composite drawings, have become valuable artifacts beyond their informational merit.

The scope of this book is to deal with the strength of these composite graphics in design presentation. A significant portion of the book also gives examples of composite drawings from contemporary architects in Australia, Japan, Malaysia and the United States. It should be noted that the drawings in this book were drawn before the construction of a building, or in some cases for unrealized buildings. Such drawings often play an important role in the development of architectural ideas and new movements, and they are significantly different from drawings that merely present a building after it is finished.

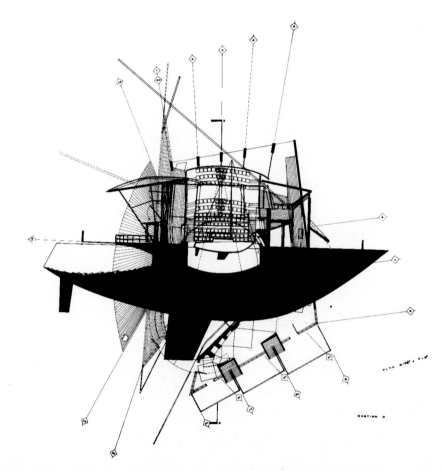

Figure 01: The logical fusion of plan and section drawings (during the design development process), results in experimental hybrid graphics and runs the risk of ambiguity (and could defeat the main purpose, if presented without the context of related drawings).
Drawing by Joseph Dreher, Savannah College of Art and Design. M. Saleh Uddin, Studio Critic.

THE CONCEPT OF ONE DRAWING

A conventional architectural presentation consists of a series of multi-views (plan, elevation, section) and three-dimensional, single-view drawings (paraline, perspective) which are perceived as independent, informative drawings. However, if the intention of architectural drawings is to illustrate a total project or building, then logically all architectural drawings should "read" as one drawing instead of a series of individual drawings representing segments of the building. When a composite drawing, illustrating sequential and integrated arrangement of individual drawings, is produced, the result is a dynamic and effective presentation of the total design. Composite drawings are particularly important in an academic environment because students often present their drawings as individual pieces of information without prior thought of their arrangement or their relationship to each other. Requiring students to submit a design project as one composite drawing encourages planning the presentation beforehand and an increased comprehension of the total scope of the presentation.

A good layout requires a good design scheme. In all composite drawings, the following points are important considerations:

- composition based on the relationships among the drawings
- attention to primary and secondary drawings
- determination of hierarchy to reinforce emphasis and clarity
- confirmation of the substance of design content
- creation of the degree of abstraction
- selection of the graphic techniques

Since presentation drawings are not working or construction drawings, all of the drawings should have clear cross-reference between one drawing to another. The direct working relationship between the plan and the elevation creates a logical opportunity to combine the two drawings so that they cross back and forth, one to the other. The simplest method of combining two drawings into one is to draw two orthographic drawings at the same scale and to arrange them within close proximity of each other in a visual field of figure-ground. This technique eliminates the effect of two images "floating around" on the page and introduces a third ground as the connector for both drawings.

The fusion of two or more drawings results in experimental hybrid graphics with variations in scale, type of drawing, reprographic technique and the use of repetition and overlapping elements. Although a large number of diverse drawings combined into one drawing runs the risk of serious ambiguity (and could defeat the main purpose), composite drawings offer opportunities to explore and experiment with the presentation, to emphasize, de-emphasize, compose and decompose specific parts of a design drawing (figure 01).

Architectural competitions have been a fertile field for composite drawings. Significant experimentation with layout is noticeable in recent architectural competition projects where each participant tries to arrange the maximum amount of information within a limited area of space. According to Tom Porter, "a major influence on this experimentation has been the growth of the international design competition and the subsequent publication of prize winners in design journals. As a result of the competition restriction on size and number of sheets, and the designer's need to catch the judge's eye in preliminary rounds of selection, this more dynamic and adventurous approach to layout design has evolved. The competition layout is characterized by considerable variation in the scale of drawings and the squeezing together, overlapping and layering of graphic information within the format. Such layouts are carefully orchestrated, being reminiscent of how an artist might plan an abstract composition. Indeed, the assembly of a series of multi-view fragments into the frozen dynamic of a large and complex layout has obvious roots in Cubism and Constructivism."

HISTORICAL OVERVIEW

In the early days, words were used for building simple structures. For complicated buildings, to give a brief and accurate description of the construction, it became necessary to explain the ideas through pictorial methods. The first incident of such pictorial method was recorded in an architectural hieroglyph of ancient Egypt (4400-2466 BC).

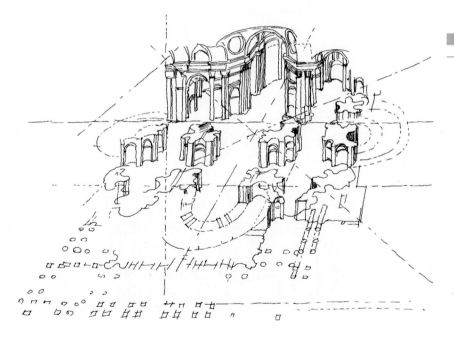

Figure 02: The sectional perspective of St. Peter's in Rome illustrates the plan, section and interior perspective in the same drawing creating various layers of information. Redrawn by author after Peruzzi's drawing.

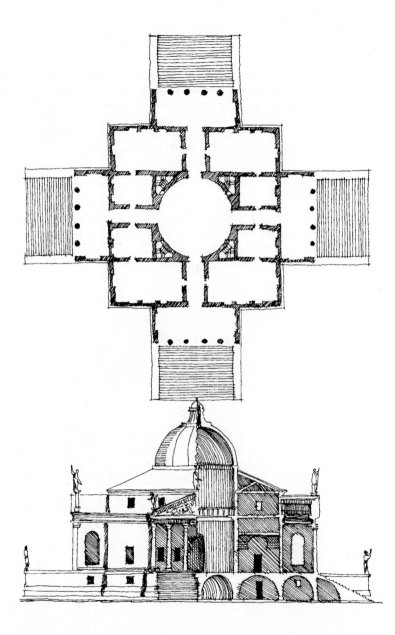

Figure 03: Andrea Palladio's illustration in woodcut for La Rotunda (Quattro Libri, 1570) shows the arrangement of plan and elevation-section in a simple cross-referential manner. The drawing reveals more information by the fusion of elevation and section drawing in the same elevation profile. Redrawn by author after Palladio's woodcut drawing.

Although there are many references to a developed system of architectural drawing in ancient Greece, none of those drawings have survived. At that time architectural plans were classified as temporary and probably were drawn on perishable materials. Also there is not much evidence of Roman drawings, even though the complexity of their buildings suggests that drawings must have been used in construction. Between the fall of the Roman Empire and the year 1000, many buildings, particularly cathedrals, were based on geometrical calculations for which drawings were not necessary. It is assumed that the builders of the medieval period were far more capable than we are today of thinking out large structures in three dimensions.

The late Fifteenth Century Italian architects Bramante and Peruzzi were the first to design in perspective. The sectional perspective of St. Peter's, Rome, illustrates the plan, section and interior perspective in the same drawing creating various layers of information (figure 02). Giovanni Battista Piranesi produced many imaginative and analytical drawings like The Baths of Caracalla (1756) showing both plan and elevation in the same layout. During the Italian Renaissance, the invention of the printing press, the extensive use of paper, and the development of an understanding of perspectives facilitated the exchange of architectural ideas through books. Other new media in the Sixteenth Century includes extensive woodcut drawings and copperplate engraving for architectural drawing. Andrea Palladio's illustration in woodcut for La Rotunda (Quattro Libri, 1570) shows the arrangement of plan and elevation-section in a simple cross-referential manner. The drawing reveals more information by the fusion of elevation and section drawing in the same elevation profile (figure 03).

Although developed delineation had been in existence in Italy during the Fifteenth Century, the architects of France and England did not follow for some time. Many early delineation works in England show the use of pen and line with wash, illustrating more effective communication by the fusion of elevations and sections or other drawings into one integrated drawing. This type of drawing gives a clear cross-reference to related details and is capable of explaining both the interior and exterior, without distorting the overall form of the building.

MODERN AND CONTEMPORARY TRENDS

Two schools with international influence, the Ecole des Beaux Arts Institute in Paris and the Bauhaus in Germany, offered designers opposing views regarding design theory and architectural presentation. At the Ecole des Beaux Arts, design and delineation were equally important, and delineation was considered as an entity within itself, separate from the design concept. On the other hand, the Bauhaus used delineation as a tool to accentuate the more important aspects of the design concept. Later, modernism or international style advocated the continuation of Bauhaus ideas, disregarding the Ecole des Beaux Arts predilection for drawings as art.

Even though modernism patronized straightforward, informative, separate drawings, some architects continued to place value on the pleasing presentation of their work. In many cases, the quality of the architectural drawing stood out only on those projects where getting the building constructed was not a serious consideration. While breaking away from the pragmatist tradition of the fifties, many new ideas became unveiled through visions for an architectural utopia. Archigram in England and the Metabolists in Japan and Vienna, suggested a complete, attainable environment in their drawings rather than representing the structure to be built.

In its departure from modernism, the Post-Modern period introduced new intentions toward architectural drawing. Aldo Rossi in Milan, Oswald Mathias Ungers in Berlin, Raimund Abraham and Rob Krier in Vienna, and Leon Krier in London all emphasized the relative independence of architectural drawings and led to a new aesthetic which eventually became recognized in its own right. Among American architects, Charles Moore, Michael Graves, John Hejduk, Robert Venturi, Steven Holl and Peter Eisenman are the pioneers. Most of the New-Age architects did not conceive of drawings merely as documents for construction. Rather drawings were seen as a medium of expression for igniting a new agenda for architecture. In addition, the emphasis of drawing by Douglas Darden, Richard Ferrier, Steven Holl, House+House, Frank Israel, Helmut Jahn, Morphosis, Eric Owen Moss, Carlo Scarpa, and Bernard Tschumi in many instances seems to communicate information through a nonconventional means of drawing interpretation.

Douglas Darden's "Dis/continuous Genealogies" for the project McMillan Water Filtration Plant represents a composite conceptualization of iconography, structure, formal composition and program of the architectural project. This incorporates a process of developing design from logic and findings (figure 04).

Richard B. Ferrier's composite "Windows and Fragments - the Picturesque" is a conceptual drawing referring to investigation and exploration for a juxtaposition of architectural considerations. The landscape, layered images, fragments and windows offer insights toward a new reality. Tension and contradictory elements are frequently explored to force an alternative response. The composition is incrementally developed to avoid preconception (figure 05).

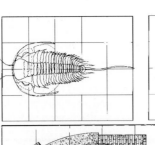
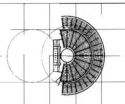
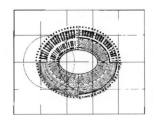
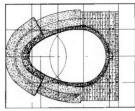
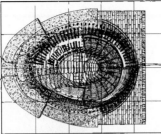

Dis/continuous Genealogy
Middle Cambrian Trilobite
Theater at Epidaurus
Coliseum at Rome
Washington Main Water Culvert
Composite Ideogram

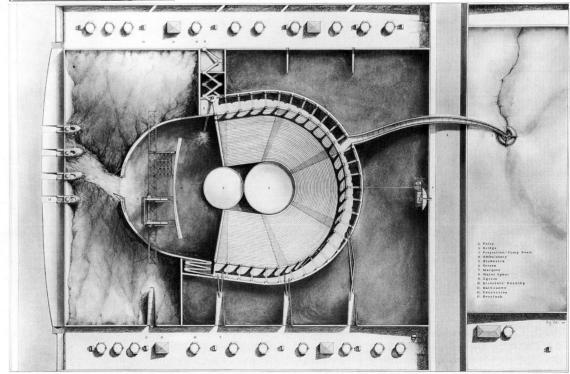

Figure 04: Douglas Darden's "Dis/continuous Genealogies" represents a composite conceptualization of iconography, structure, formal composition and program of the architectural project. This encorporates a process of developing design from logic and findings.

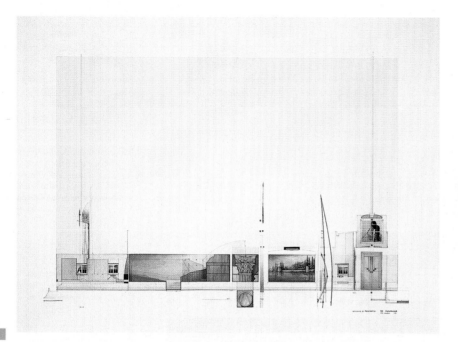

Figure 05: Richard B. Ferrier's composite "Windows and Fragments - the Picturesque" is a conceptual drawing referring to investigation and exploration for a juxtaposition of architectural considerations.

The composite presentation for the Kerby Residence by House+House illustrates as a collage of geometries, scales, and media arranged to represent the interaction between the very graphic building form and the natural setting (figure 06).

Franklin D. Israel's drawing for Limelight Productions combines and projects drawings one upon another to register the events of a sequence and to convey the many elements and various spaces of this building (figure 07).

The proposal by Helmut Jahn for the St. Paul Convention Center and Hotel shows a new approach toward a three-dimensional composite graphic presentation. It is a collage of various types of drawings summarizing the concept of the design on scroll, in the form of a reel on acrylic glass spools (figure 08). His imaginative drawing of the State of Illinois Center, Chicago (figure 09), shows the floor plan and cross section with an opened courtyard roof, an excellent example of composite delineation. For Helmut Jahn composite drawings are more like unfolding a model to reveal various concerns of a design in one drawing. In many of his drawings, rays and beams of light represent the energy and interaction of natural light within the building and the building light emitting outward from within (front cover illustration).

The drawing for Gymnasium-Bridge by Steven Holl (figure 10) is a bold but simple cross-referential drawing where elevation is composed with the plans to create a comprehensive view. The landscape layer of the site plan is used as the background layer for both of the drawings.

For Eric Owen Moss, the composite drawings are a manifestation and record of the changes and amendments as the project evolves. The composite drawings are made to provide a comprehensive understanding of the buildings from start to finish, from all angles. While they

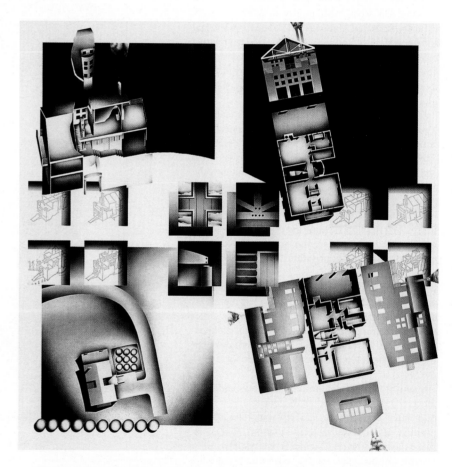

Figure 06: The composite presentation for the Kerby Residence by Mark English of House+House illustrates as a collage of geometries, scales and media arranged to represent the interaction between the very graphic building form and the natural setting.

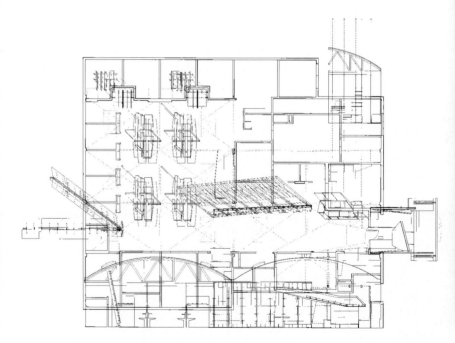

Figure 07: Franklin D. Israel's drawing for Limelight Productions combines and projects drawings one upon another to register the events of a sequence and to convey the many elements and various spaces of this building.

Figure 08: The proposal by Helmut Jahn for the St. Paul Convention Center and Hotel is a collage of various types of drawings summarizing the concept of the design on scroll, in the form of a reel on acrylic glass spools.

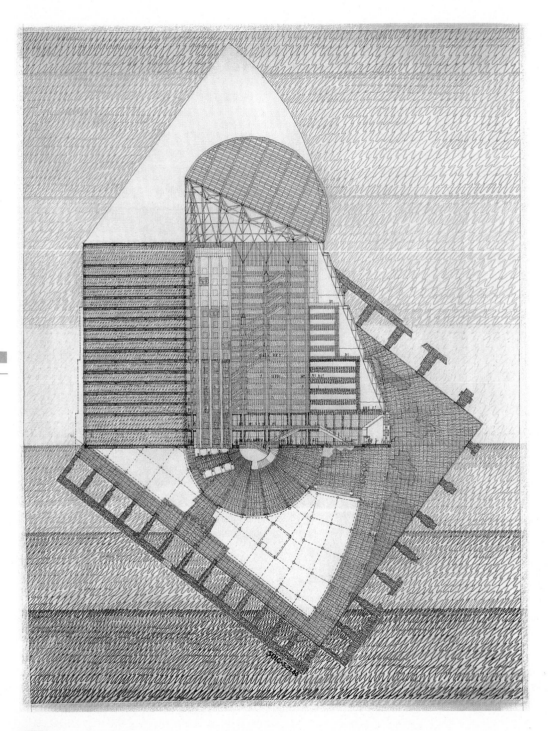

Figure 09: State of Illinois Center, Chicago, by Helmut Jahn shows the floor plan and cross section with an opened courtyard roof, an excellent example of composite delineation.

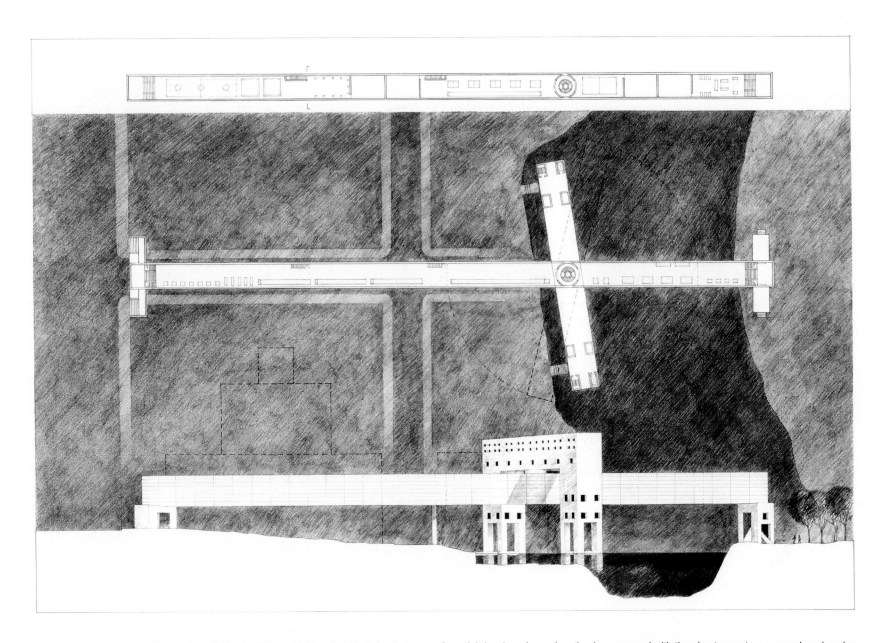

Figure 10: The drawing for Gymnasium-Bridge by Steven Holl is a bold but simple cross-referential drawing where elevation is composed with the plan to create a comprehensive view.

have an intrinsic beauty in themselves, their main function is to inform thoroughly. The rotational section views for the Indigent Pavilion (figure 11) and the split worm's eye axonometric for Lawson/Westen House (see exploratory drawing in the next chapter) almost create a full 360° rotational view which otherwise would be impossible to show with conventional single-view drawing.

Barnard Tschumi's drawing for the Parc de la Villette in Paris (figure 12) shows effective superimposition of lines, points and surfaces emphasizing the layers of landscape and built elements.

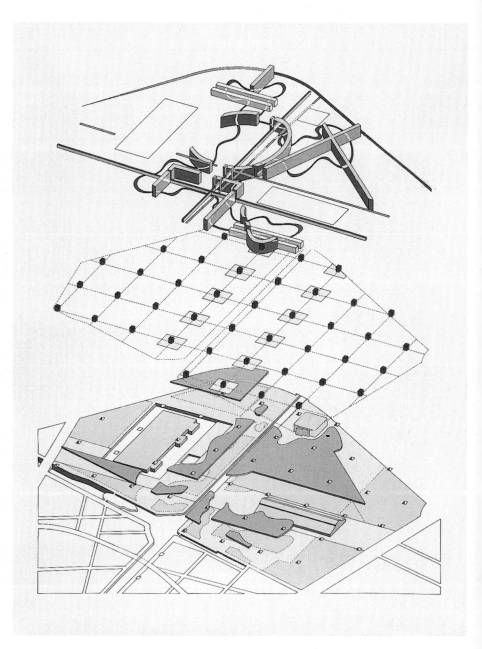

Figure 11: The rotational section views for the Indigent Pavilion by Eric Owen Moss almost creates a full 360° rotational view.

Figure 12: Barnard Tschumi's drawing for the Parc de la Villette in Paris shows effective superimposition of lines, points and surfaces emphasizing the layers of landscape and built elements.

A series of composite superimposition of plans and elevations drawings by Morphosis for the Comprehensive Cancer Center in Los Angeles (figure 13) illustrates the rotation of the moving element at different angular orientation and exploration of the fourth dimension, time. This creates a visual image of movement inclining toward an animation effect. A series of section drawings, taken in a particular sequence by Morphosis for the Lawrence House (figure 14), shows us a three-dimensional animated effect, suggesting the possibility of a strip of motion picture illusion.

The composite drawing has changed our perception and expectations of the role of architectural drawing. Although it communicates on many levels beyond utility, it is also perceived as artwork, a prized artifact that endures beyond the completion of a project. Contemporary influence of composite hybrid graphics suggests that designers will learn a new method of reading and drawing the fourth dimension, acknowledging the nonstationary nature of architectural views.

These examples, as well as drawings in the professional portfolio section, speak of the significant changes occurring in architectural representation. The power and effectiveness of multi-layered expression of composite graphics make this new form a presence too important to be ignored.

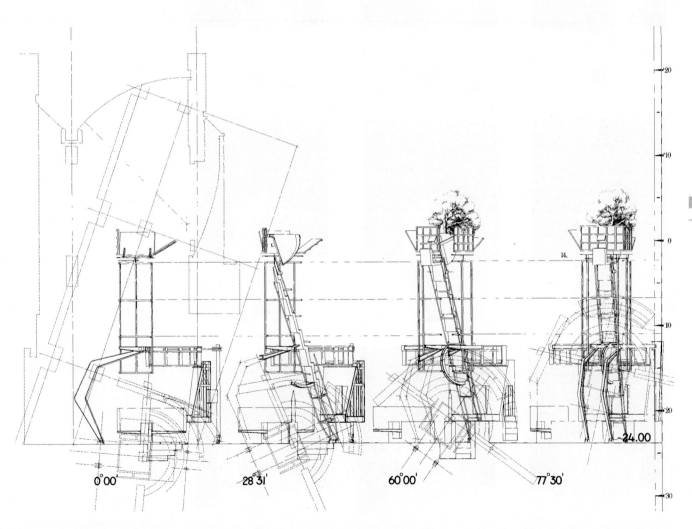

Figure 13: A series of composite superimposition of plans and elevations drawings by Morphosis for the Comprehensive Cancer Center in Los Angeles illustrates the rotation of the moving element at different angular orientation and exploration of the fourth dimension, time.

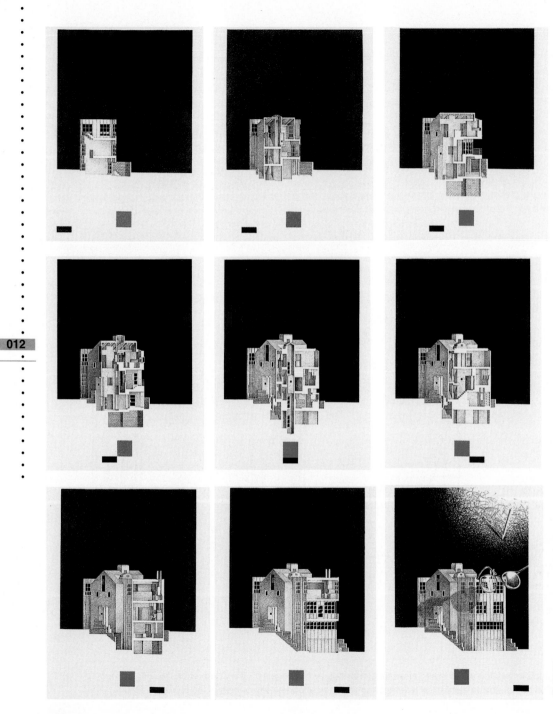

Figure 14: A series of section drawings, taken in a particular sequence by Morphosis for the Lawrence House, shows a three-dimensional animated effect, suggesting the possibility of a strip of motion picture illusion.

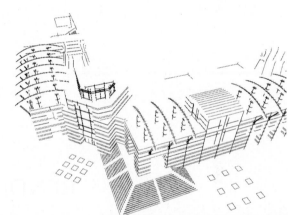

Media and Drawing Exploration ■

Rendering Techniques
Nonconventional Drawing Media
Exploratory Drawing
Media Appropriateness

RENDERING TECHNIQUES

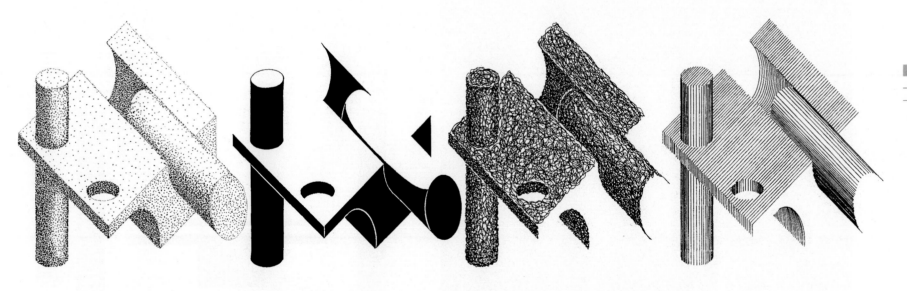

Basic rendering techniqes using technical pen and black ink. Dots, high contrast, scribbles and lines.
Kendrick Harrison (Student), Southern University. M. Saleh Uddin, Studio Professor.

RENDERING TECHNIQUES

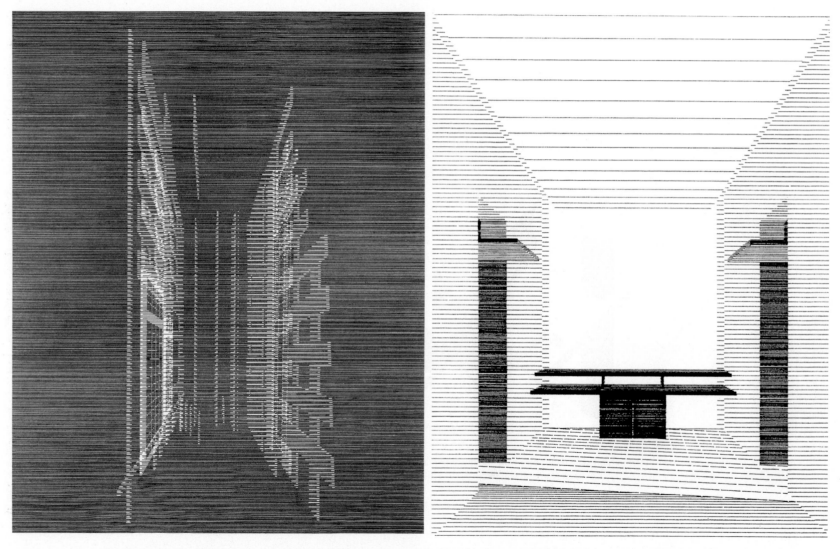

Interior perspective. Hand-drawn in lead pencil on Japanese paper. Drawings showing composition of spaces by the layering of walls.
Takefumi Aida, Tokyo, Japan. GKD Building, Hiroshima, Japan, and Tokyo War Dead Memorial Park, Tokyo, Japan.

RENDERING TECHNIQUES

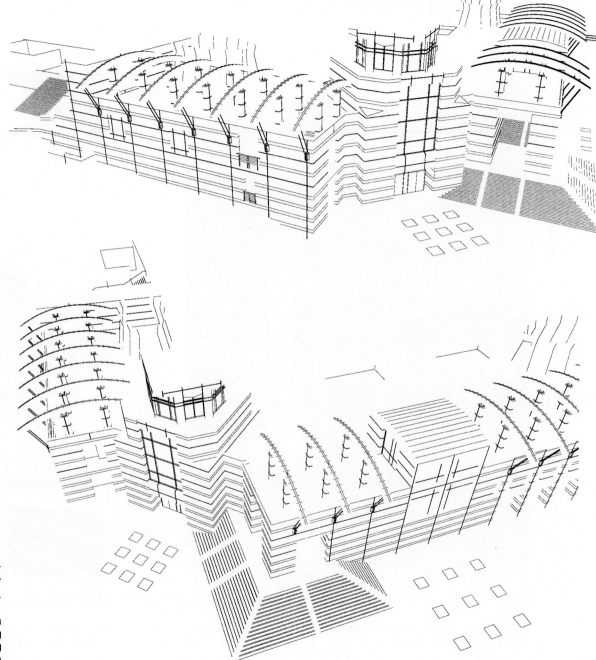

Shadowed axonometrics. Drawing technique emphasizes the building elements (screeds, stairs, window frames, etc.) in shadow lines. Drawn on AutoCAD.

R. L. Binder, FAIA, California
Drawn by Chilin Huang
UCLA, Ackerman Student Union Building
Los Angeles, California

RENDERING TECHNIQUES

Technical pen and ink on mylar. Rendering with lines, dots, scribbles and solid black.
Tariano Davis (Student), Howard University
John Chen, Studio Professor

Technical pen and ink on white vellum. Only dots and solid black used in rendering. No lines to create edges.
Joseph Anthony (Student), Southern University
M. Saleh Uddin, Studio Professor

Rendering of Le Corbusier's Palace of Assembly portico, Chandigarh, India. Left drawing: Technical pen and ink on white vellum. Only dots used in rendering. No lines used to create edges. Right drawing: Pen and ink on airbrush rendering using black acrylic paint.
Sean Turner (Student), Southern University. M. Saleh Uddin, Studio Professor.

Elevation. Graphite powder, gouache, and pastel on
Stonehenge paper.
Douglas Darden, Associate Professor
University of Colorado, Denver, Colorado
Oxygen House, Mississippi

Perspective. Charcoal on Silverhill Kent paper.
Riken Yamamoto + Field Shop, Yokohama, Japan. Inner-Junction City, Yokohama, Japan.

RENDERING TECHNIQUES

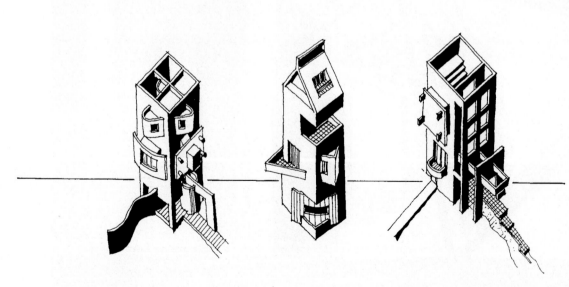

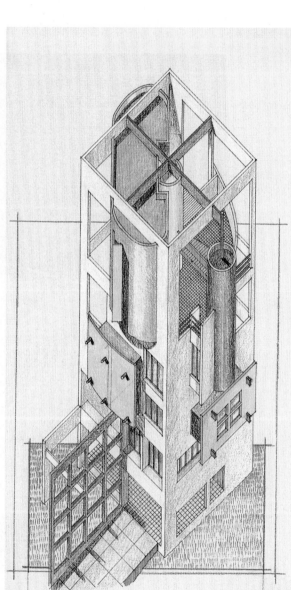

Freehand study sketches with technical pen on sketch paper. More developed axonometric using prismacolor pencil on ink line drawing. M. Saleh Uddin. Scheme for a House.

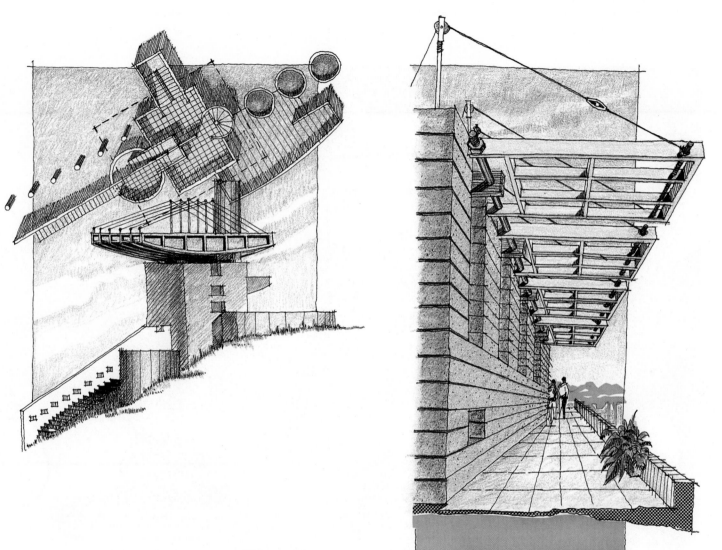

Freehand study sketches. Sketch outlined in pencil and black felt-tipped pen, colored with prismacolor pencil. Framing portion of background sky helps accentuate specific areas of the scheme.
M. Saleh Uddin.

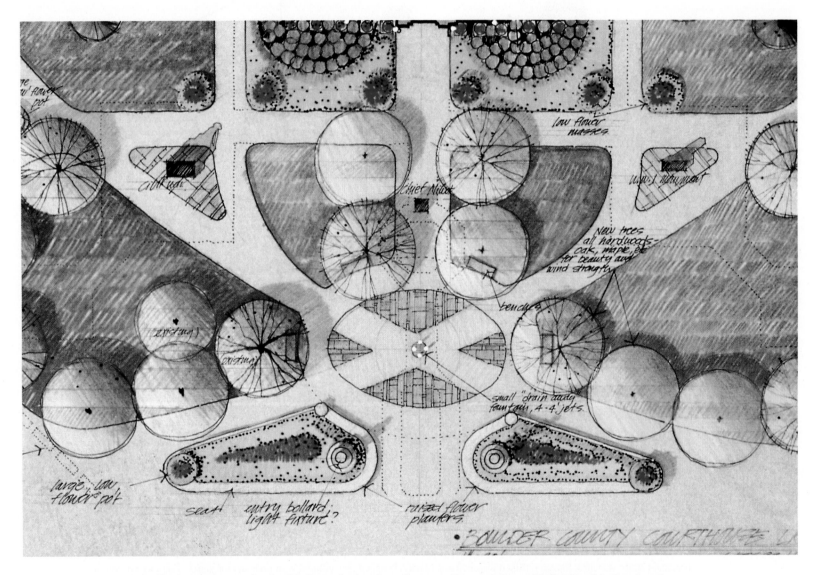

Rendering landscape elements in plan. Marker and colored pencil on trace line work done with fine-line felt-tipped marker.
Boulder County Courthouse lawn, Boulder, Colorado. Michael E. Doyle, Communication Arts, Inc., Colorado.

PERSPECTIVE · LINEAR OASIS STUDY

Colored pencil over alcohol marker on photocopy bond paper.
Arch across Post Oak Boulevard, Houston, Texas. Michael E. Doyle, Communication Arts, Inc., Colorado.

RENDERING TECHNIQUES

Colored pencil over photocopied image on Canson paper.
Study for Maguire Thomas Partners, Los Angeles, California. Michael E. Doyle, Communication Arts, Inc., Colorado.

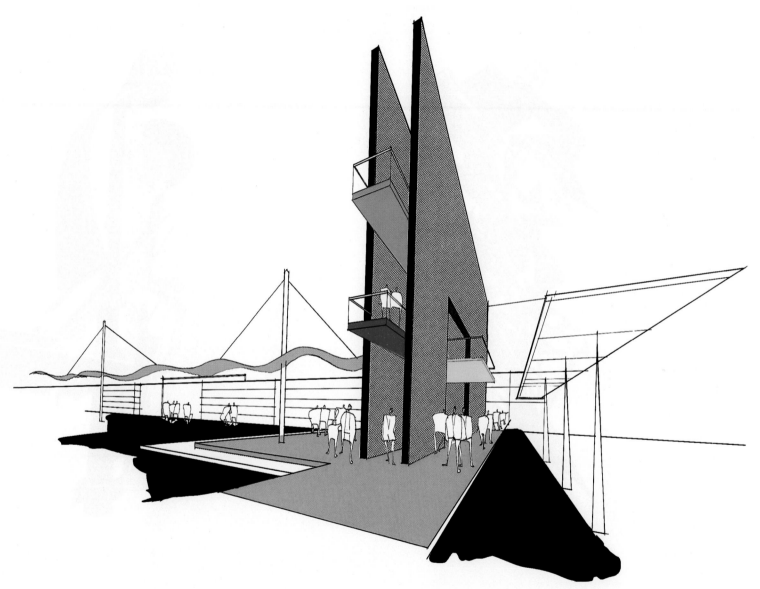

Exterior perspective. Pen and ink tracing paper base drawing copied on .3 mm clear acetate sheet. Adhesive dot screen and color adhesive film applied on clear acetate print to create this preliminary design sketch.

Hong Park, Professor, Chung-Ang University, Seoul, Korea. Memorial Tower, Student's Park, Chung-Ang University, Seoul, Korea.

RENDERING TECHNIQUES

Prismacolor pencil highlight on pen and ink drawing.
John Biron (Student), Savannah College of Art and Design
M. Saleh Uddin, Studio Critic
Entry-Path-Place

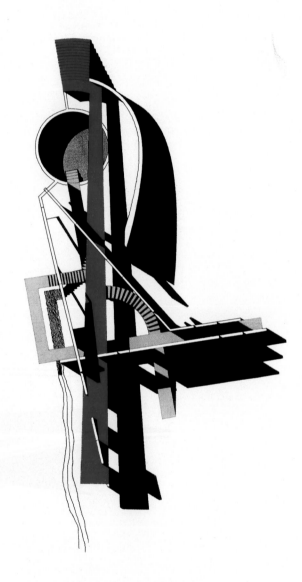

Color adhesive film on pen and ink drawing.
Frederic Amey (Student), Savannah College of Art and Design
M. Saleh Uddin, Studio Critic
Entry-Path-Place

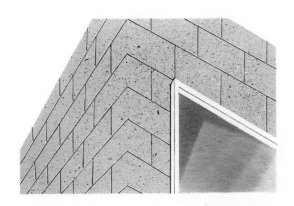

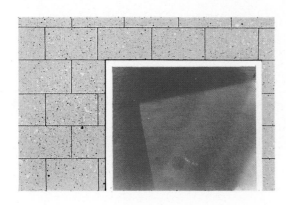

029

Rendering surface texture of brick and concrete. Airbrush and acrylic paint. Mortar joints drawn with technical pen using both black and white ink.
Mindy Kauffman, John Cooksey (Students), Savannah College of Art and Design. M. Saleh Uddin, Studio Professor.

RENDERING TECHNIQUES

Spray paint on ink line drawing on 30"x40" mylar. Coarse grains of $1.00 waterproof spray paint reproduce better than fine grain airbrush technique, since dots are visible. Exterior perspective of a penetrating I-beam entry canopy.

Ronn W. Yong, Ohio. Lorenzo Carter Building, Warehouse District Cleveland, Ohio.

RENDERING TECHNIQUES

Airbrush rendering using opaque paint on white Strathmore cold press board. Black paint for rendering building interior, and blue and white paint for sky. Frisket film used for masking. 18" x 22". M. Saleh Uddin.

031

RENDERING TECHNIQUES

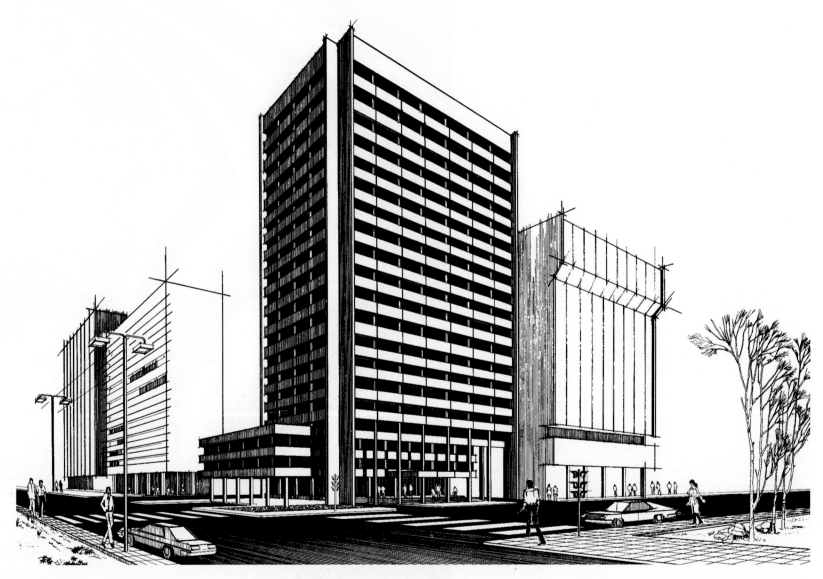

Perspective drawn from model (not from mechanical plan projection) to save time. Vanishing points established by eye estimation, looking at the desired view of the model.
Pen and ink on white vellum.
M. Saleh Uddin for Dexterous Consultants, Dhaka, Bangladesh. Head Office for Dhaka WASA.

Exterior perspective. Pen and ink base drawing rendered in water color. The perspective drawing of the building was computer generated. Environmental elements and context were hand drawn. Pen and ink was chosen in order to create a very detailed and precise base drawing. The final phase of the drawing was created by transferring the pen and ink drawing to watercolor paper and then adding transparent watercolor. The desired effect is a realistic yet inviting image that communicates the design in a clear and precise manner.

Ellerbe Becket, Los Angeles; Art Zendarski, Renderer. San Diego Hall of Justice Competition, San Diego, California.

RENDERING TECHNIQUES

Exterior perspective. Airbrush and embellished by hand on 3D generated in Macintosh MacArchitrion, drawn with a pencil plotter by Mutoh on 30"x40" vellum.
Charles Graves & Ronn W. Yong, Ohio. French House, Twin Lakes, Ohio

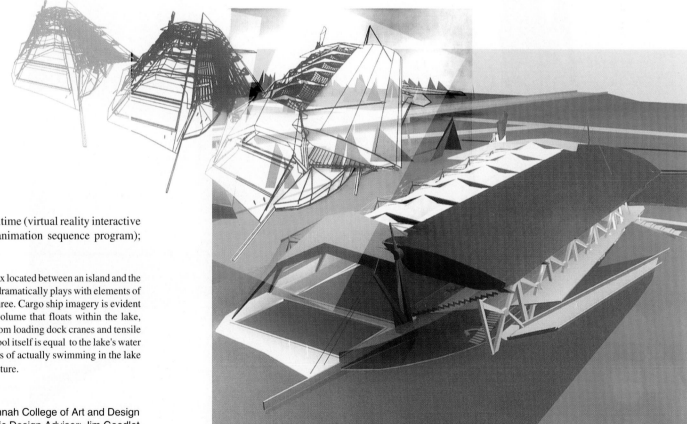

DataCad (3D design); StereoCad Realtime (virtual reality interactive application); Autodesk 3D Studio (animation sequence program); Adobe Photoshop (color renderings).

An Olympic natatorium and diving complex located between an island and the shore of a man-made lake in a public park dramatically plays with elements of land, sea and air as it hovers between all three. Cargo ship imagery is evident in the concept of a container for liquid volume that floats within the lake, protected by a skeletal structure derived from loading dock cranes and tensile fabric enclosures. The water level of the pool itself is equal to the lake's water level creating the sensation for competitors of actually swimming in the lake within the floating framework of the structure.

Drew Miller (Student), Savannah College of Art and Design
Studio Critic: Deirdre Hardy, Electronic Design Advisor: Jim Goodlet
Olympic Natatorium, Lake Mayer, Georgia

RENDERING TECHNIQUES

3D model generated in AT&T Topas. Several objects are semi-transparent, allowing a depth in the drawing that is not easily attained through other techniques. TGA format images taken into Adobe Photoshop for manipulation as necessary on a Macintosh platform.

Keelan P. Kaiser (Student),
University of Nebraska-Lincoln.
Alexander Maller, Studio Critic.
A Center for the Study of
Television and Film.

NONCONVENTIONAL DRAWING MEDIA
EXPLORATORY DRAWING
MEDIA APPROPRIATENESS

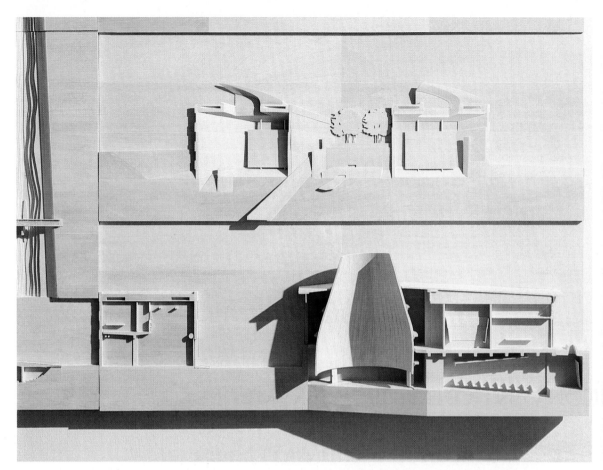

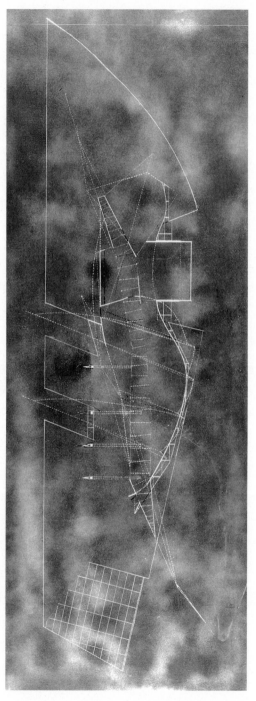

NONCONVENTIONAL DRAWING MEDIA

RELIEF WOOD DRAWING

Relief drawing in bass wood. Combination of model making technique and drawing.
Tod Williams Billie Tsien and Associates, New York. Los Angeles Art Park, Los Angeles, California.

ETCHING

Conceptual floor plan. Etching on 11"x4" aluminum. Acid and selenium oxide applied to a sheet of aluminum to produce a surface patina. A carbide etching tool is used to pull away the patina and reveal the layer of raw aluminum below.
E. J. Meade (Student), University of Colorado. Douglas Darden, Studio Critic. School for the Teaching of Building Trades.

NONCONVENTIONAL DRAWING MEDIA

MIXED MEDIA/COLLAGE

A wide variety of materials include masonite board, corrugated brown board, plexiglass, gesso, metal screen, sepia copy, acetate drawings and burnt drawings. Part of a ten-board presentation (each board 40"x40") represents the nature of nuclear devastation awareness and disarmament.

Lee S. Mengt (Student)
University of Southwestern Louisiana
George S. Loli, and Dan Branch, Studio Critics
Nuclear Disarmament Center, Washington, D.C.

039

NONCONVENTIONAL DRAWING MEDIA

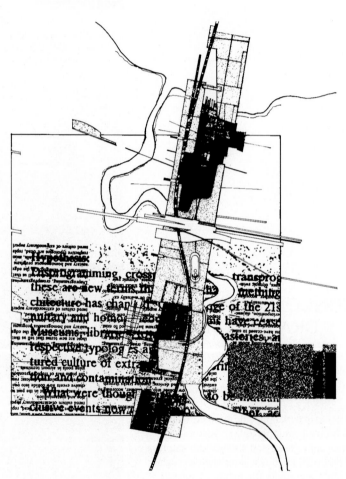

USE OF TEXT

Text extracted from the program as well as key words of the design concept photocopied at various scale and intensity to create texture and grain in the drawing. Text surface capable of creating additional visual layer and informative layer.

Ronn W. Yong + Sharlene Young, Ohio. 'Urbanconnector' Linear City.

NONCONVENTIONAL DRAWING MEDIA

SWISS CHOCOLATE

Toblorone Swiss chocolate applied with spatula on smooth Canson paper. Monochrome sepia-like color brings translucent quality against light source. Media appropriate for imaginative ideas rather than specific details where controlled lines and edges are not important.

George S. Loli, Associate Professor
University of Southwestern Louisiana

EXPLORATORY DRAWING

Synthesis drawing using all of the three basic projection types (orthographic, axonometric and perspective) all constructed from one another.

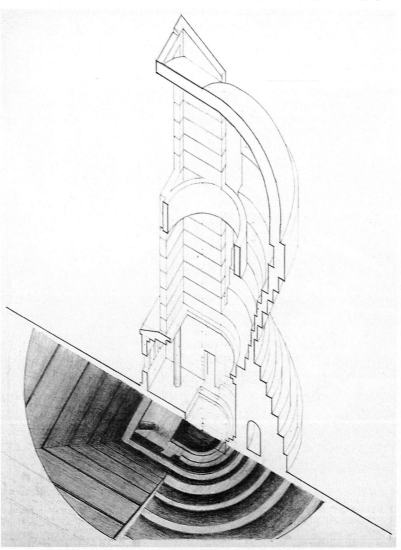

A down-view perspective looking at the floor of the space in tone, and a plan oblique projection of one-half of the project, both made from the plan at the center. The project was a one room space for a Tower to the Winds.

Bruce Brunner (Student), University of Arkansas. Randall Ott, Studio Critic.

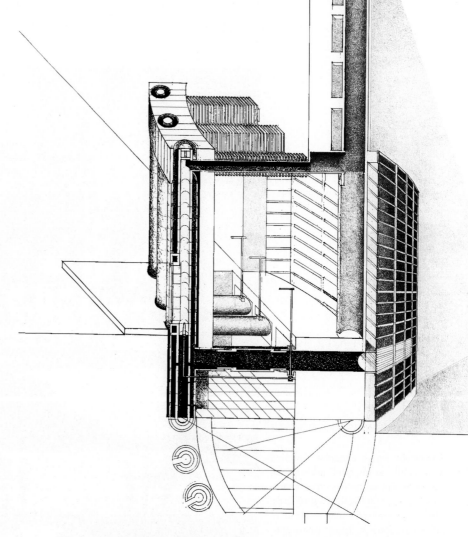

The design is for a hearth, and the intention was to take a wall section through the hearth and draw an interior section oblique projection and an exterior one-point perspective.

Jason Landrum (Student), University of Arkansas. Randall Ott, Studio Critic.

EXPLORATORY DRAWING

This synthesis drawing begins with a section cut through the main room, and a one-point interior perspective is cast within the room. A one-point exterior perspective showing a portion of how the building would look from the street is attached to the section cut on the right-hand side. A down-view section oblique projection is then made of the room from the exterior, attaching to the original section. The lower rooms shown in the section are section-oblique. The project was for a Prytaneion--an ancient Greek building type where the eternal flame was kept burning. The main space is the Flame Hall.

Mark Shutt (Student), University of Arkansas. Randall Ott, Studio Critic.

EXPLORATORY DRAWING

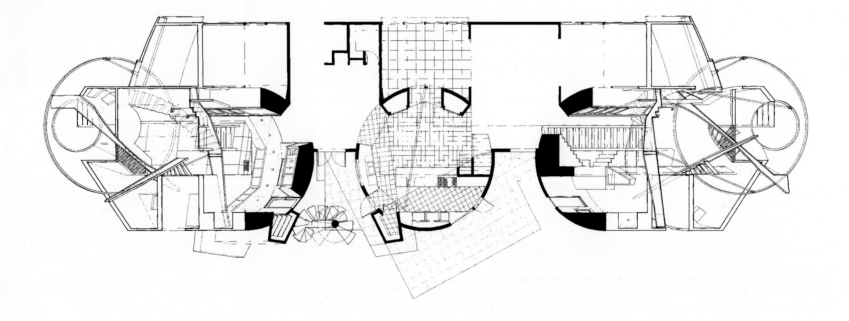

Plan with split worm's eye axonometric.

Eric Owen Moss Architects, California • Lawson/Westen House, Los Angeles, California.

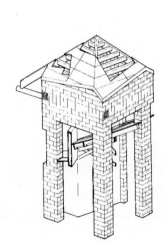

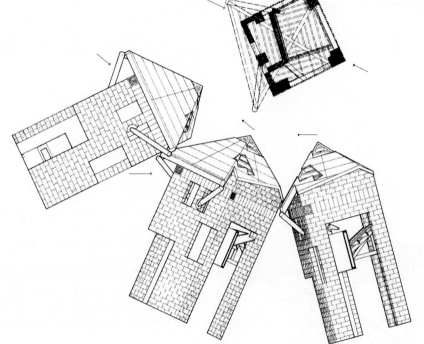

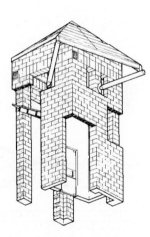

Projected plan, elevation, auxilliary, and oblique views.

Eric Owen Moss Architects, California • Lindblade Tower, Culver City, California.

EXPLORATORY DRAWING

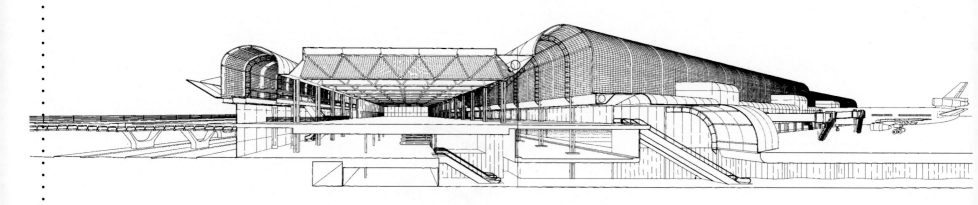

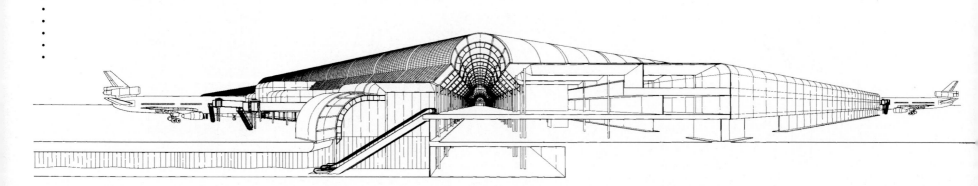

Sectional interior-exterior perspective. Split projection with multiple vanishing points.

Murphy/Jahn Architects, Illinois • United Airlines Terminal 1 Complex, O'Hare International Airport, Chicago, Illinois.

LIBRARY

Photo-sketch. Spatial representation through a combination of photographs of construction and hand drawing of created perspective (from photographs). During construction, photographic snapshots were made of interior spaces to document on-site progress. The photographs were spliced together with the remaining perspective completed as a graphite drawing.

Richard B. Ferrier, FAIA, Texas • GBC Douglas House, Lake Texamo, Texas.

MEDIA APPROPRIATENESS

One of the principal focuses of this design project was an ideological synthesis between project and its means of representation. This meant not merely that the presentation be appropriate to the ideas inherent in the project but that the representation be the project.

The final presentation drawings for this Summer Sanatorium for 14 Tuberculosis patients link the way in which the disease Tuberculosis is represented to those infected (through x-ray) and a specific condition emphasized on the project's island site (in the evening, a nearby lighthouse illuminates it from behind).

Breathing and the characteristic Tuberculosis cough are also ideas integral to both project and representation. The project itself is sited as though poised to cough, in the act of coughing, or having coughed, and the circulation upward, into, and ultimately outward from the sanatorium is done in an effort to mimic the act of breathing.

The initial chest activity and chest x-ray drawings were made with an atomizer by literally coughing ink through a tube onto the sheet. The final project drawings were all done with airbrush on mylar (a coughing/breathing machine). The final drawings were presented on a vertically mounted light table.

J. C. Smith (Student), University of Colorado
Douglas Darden, Studio Critic
Summer Sanatorium, Coast of Maine

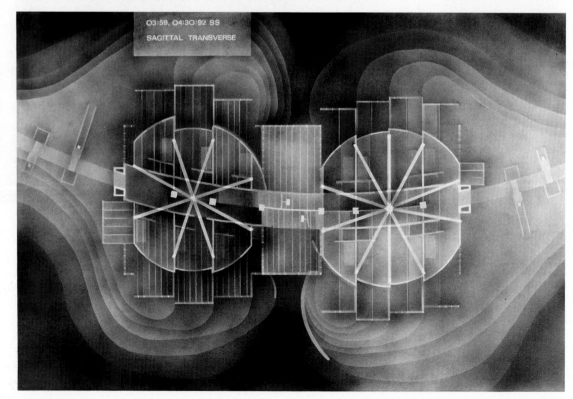

MEDIA APPROPRIATENESS

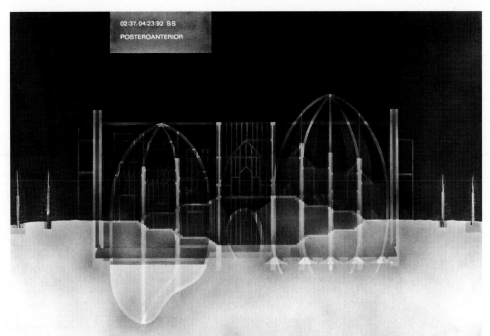

Drawings done with airbrush on mylar, representing the process of coughing-breathing. Breathing and the characteristic Tuberculosis cough are ideas integral to both project and representation.

J. C. Smith (Student), University of Colorado • Douglas Darden, Studio Critic.
Summer Sanatorium, Coast of Maine.

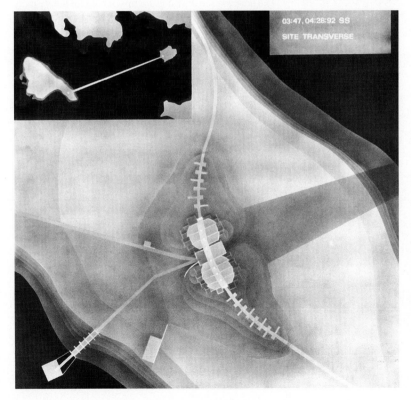

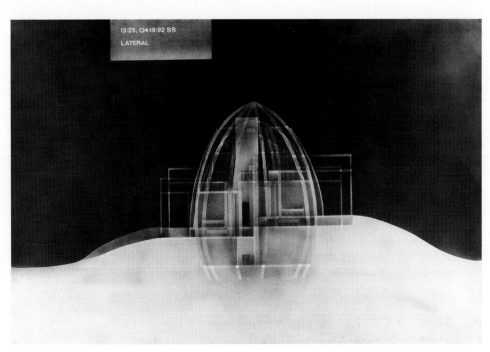

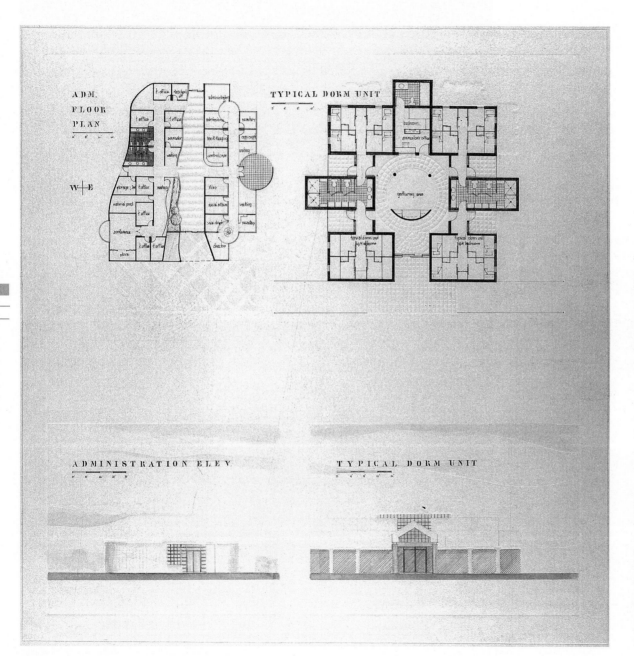

EMBOSSED DRAWING

The presentation drawings for this School for the Visually Impaired used the technique of relief and tactile texture within the drawing to make it appropriate for visually impaired readers. The representation linked the way in which an impaired reader would read a text. The project emphasized the presentation technique as being a part of the learning process of reading drawings by touching the embossed relief and recessed areas. (The only two existing things - light and darkness - cannot exist without each other. Both blend to form every existing identity. The fear of the darkness is the fear of the light as well. Between all light and shade is an object created with our minds, our hearts. The feeling of light and shade from our fingertips is as true as our desire and as true as life in our imagination.)

All nine presentation boards, each measuring 22"x22", were drawn in lead pencil with very light watercolor wash. All enclosed floor surfaces as well as interior courts and outdoor terraces were embossed with floor textures. In elevation, building edges and window openings are embossed to differentiate plane changes and glazed and nonglazed surfaces.

Maria Antonia Espinal (Student)
University of Southwestern Louisiana
George S. Loli, Studio Critic
School for the Visually Impaired, Baton Rouge, Louisiana

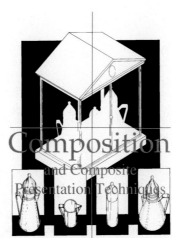

Composition and Composite Presentation Techniques

Composition and Layout
Drawings Combined in One Composition
Composite Montage

COMPOSITION AND LAYOUT

COMPOSITION

Composition in general refers to the arrangement of several elements so as to make one integrated whole, where all elements have a share in producing the whole. It is the essence of composition that everything should be in a determined place or position and perform an intended part advantageously for the whole. An intended unity, discipline and order must be the result of a good composition. This order does not necessarily refer to a formal order. In the case of architectural drawing, a good composition should always be a vehicle to express the essence of the design.

It is almost impossible to prescribe specific rules which will enable somone to compose. But there are simple laws of arrangement that would assist a designer to set forth some guidelines and interpretation for creating a composition.

Important aspects of composition for architectural design presentation are illustrated on the following pages.

FRAME OF REFERENCE

- Frame of Reference
- Figure-ground

SHAPE AND SIZE OF THE BOARD

- Narrow Rectangular Outline (Frame)
- Square Outline
- Curvilinear Outline
- Irregular Edges

FRAME OF REFERENCE

COMPOSITION AND LAYOUT

FRAME OF REFERENCE/FIGURE-GROUND

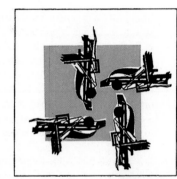

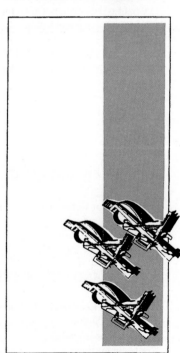

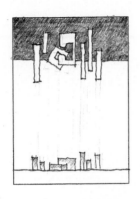

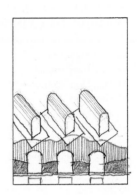

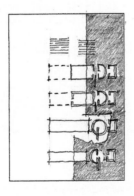
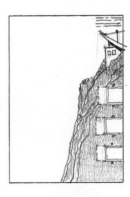
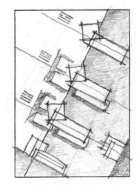
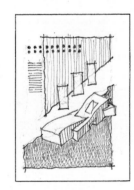

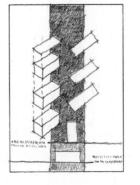
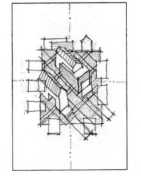
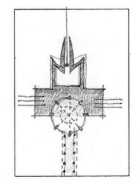

LAYOUT EMPHASIS

- Composition with Dominant Top
- Composition with Dominant Base
- Composition with Dominant Side
- Composition with Diagonal Emphasis
- Composition with Horizontal Emphasis
- Composition with Vertical Emphasis
- Composition with Focus on a Central (or Point) Area

055

COMPOSITION AND LAYOUT

PRIMARY MEANS TO COMBINE DRAWINGS

- Using Figure-ground
- Using Background
- Using Dominant Base
- Using Grid
- Using Frame
- Using Frame + Background
- Using Scale Variation
- Using Design Element

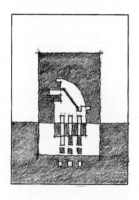
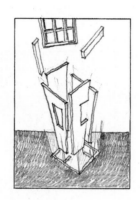
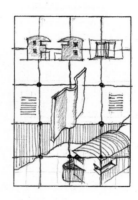
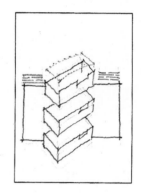

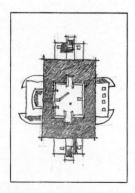
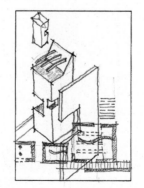
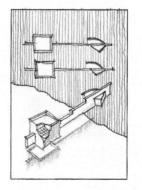
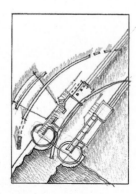

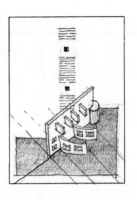

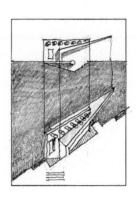
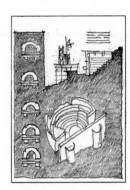

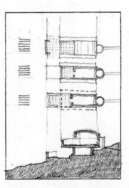
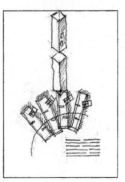
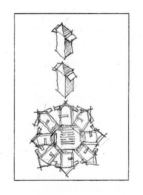
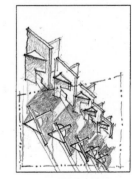

COMPOSITION MOTIF FOR TOTAL PRESENTATION

- Self-contained Composition (Singular Forms, Plural Forms, Compound Forms)
- Composition with Repetition (One-directional, Multi-directional)
- Composition with Radiation (Segmental Radiation, Full Radiation)
- Composition with Gradation (Gradation of Shape, Size, Position, Proportion)
- Composition with Similarity (Repetition, Radiation, Gradation)
- Composition with Concentration (Central, Linear, Planar Concentration)
- Composition with Contrast (Contrast of Placement, Appearance, Quantity)
- Composition with Anomaly (Anomaly in Shape, Size, Color, Texture, Position, Direction)

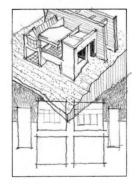
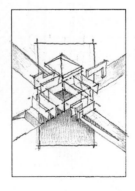
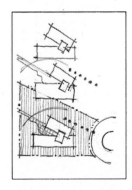

COMPOSITION AND LAYOUT

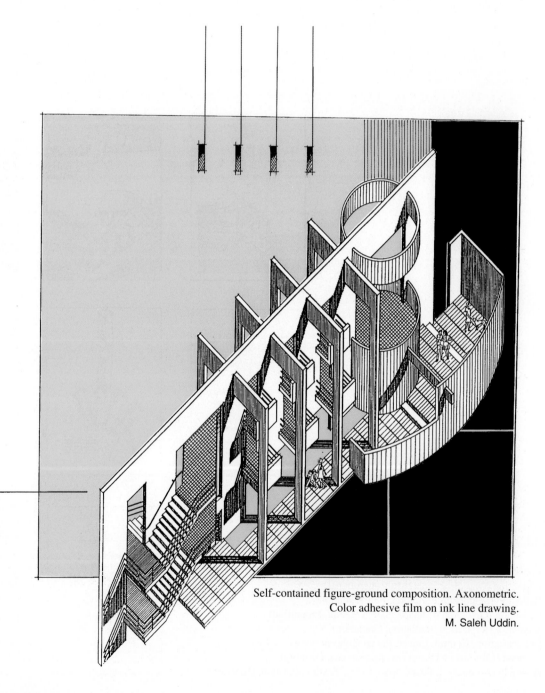

Self-contained figure-ground composition. Axonometric.
Color adhesive film on ink line drawing.
M. Saleh Uddin.

Composition with dominant top. Composition of the drawing challenges the negative space below and struggles to create an equilibrium within the drawing as part of the design concept.
Elevation. Dot screen tone overlays on ink line drawing on 14"x 17" vellum.
Ronn W. Yong + Sharlene Young, Ohio. House 27536.

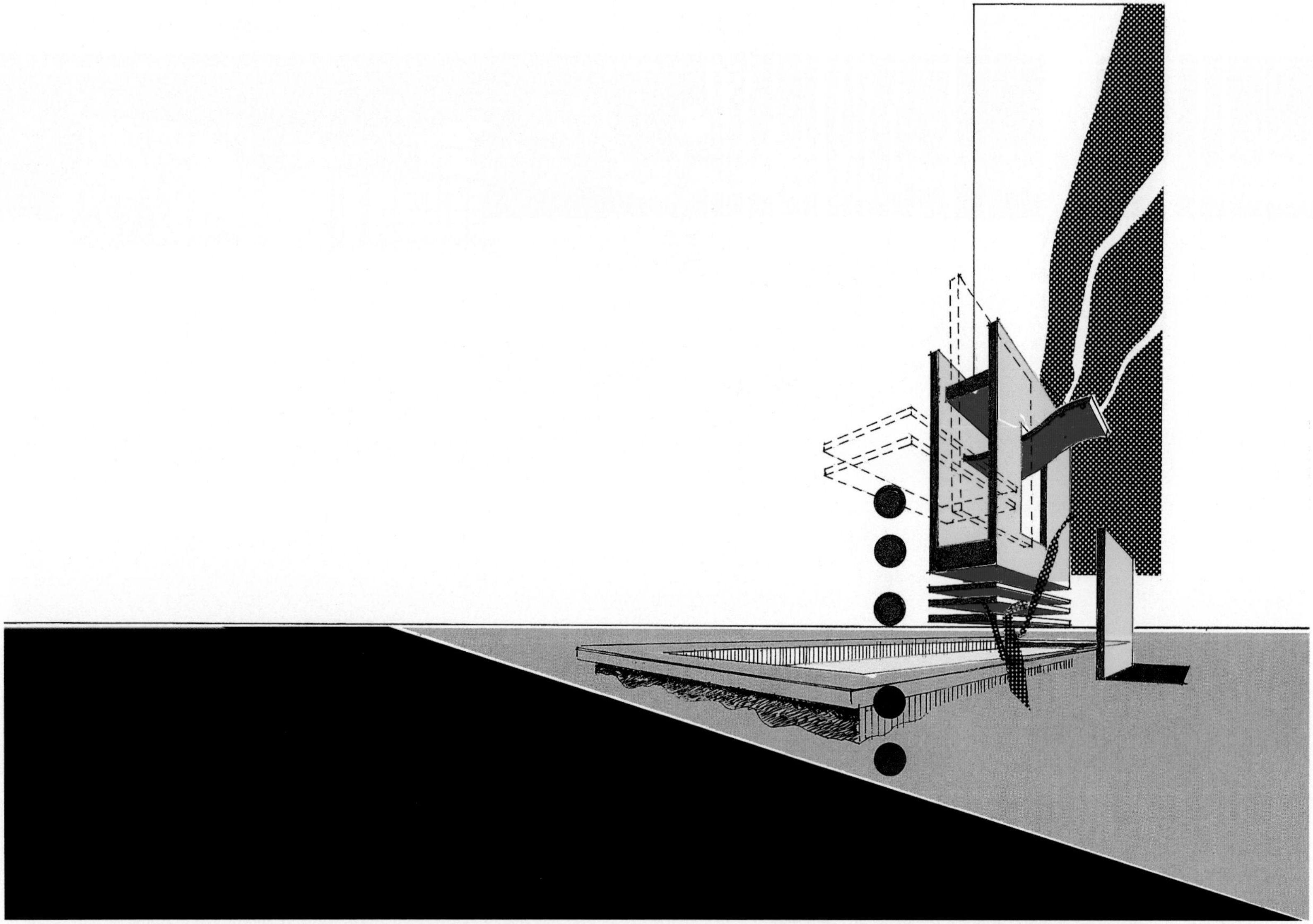

060

Composition with dominant base. Schematic perspective. Color adhesive film, dot screen and black cut paper on ink line drawing.
M. Saleh Uddin.

COMPOSITION AND LAYOUT

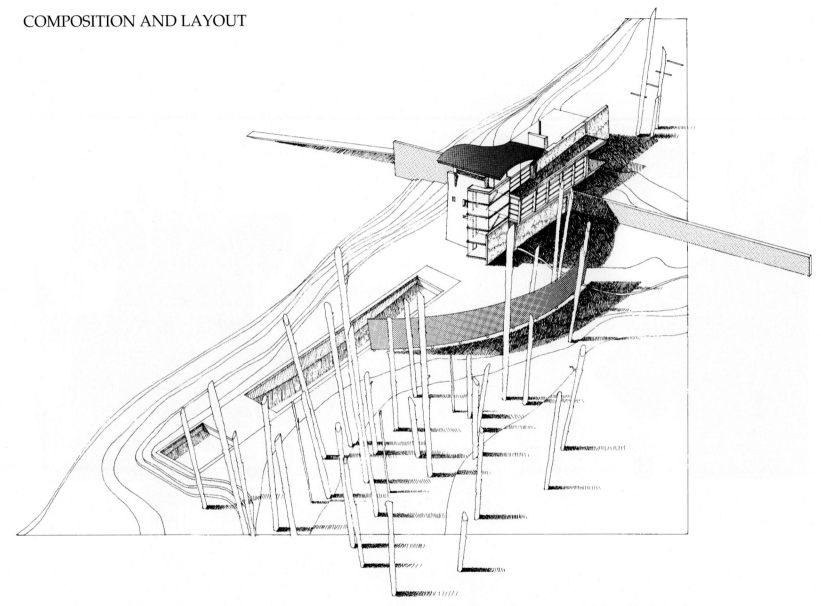

Composition with diagonal emphasis. Composition of the drawing is balanced by the emphasis of triangular negative space and violation of border on the left and on the top. Exterior aerial perspective. Dot screen tone overlays on ink line drawing on 14"x 17" vellum.
Ronn W. Yong + Sharlene Young, Ohio. House 27536.

COMPOSITION AND LAYOUT

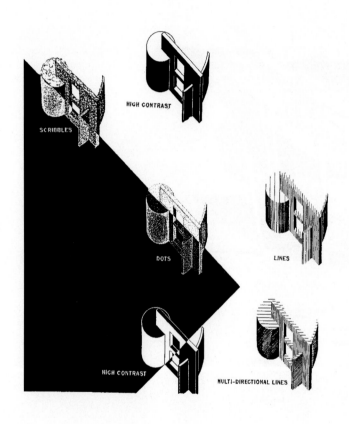

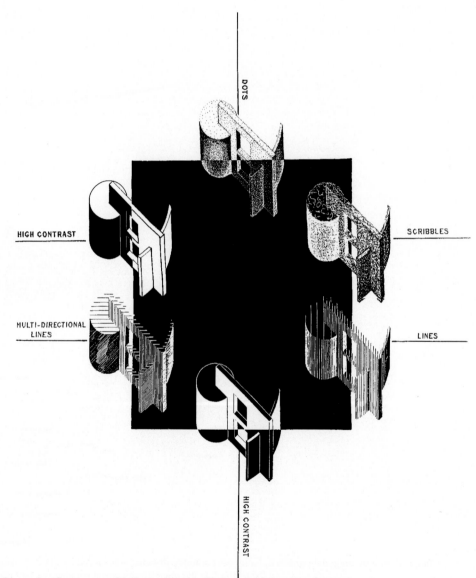

Composition using figure-ground and repetitive motif. Pen and ink on bond paper.
Shonda D. Piper (Student) Southern University.   M. Saleh Uddin, Studio Critic.

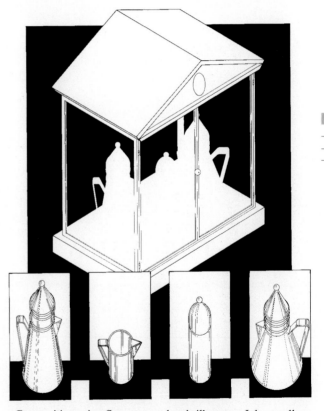

Composition using figure-ground, frame and silhouette. Freehand ink on vellum still-life sketches explore rendering techniqes using dots, lines, contrast and profile.
Deena D. Miles (Student), Southern University.
M. Saleh Uddin, Studio Critic. Still-life Sketch/Rendering Techniques.

Composition using figure-ground and silhouette. Ink on vellum axonometric drawing analyzes the design into its elemental parts and their relationships.
Donald Burke (Student), Savannah College of Art and Design.
Andrew Chandler, Studio Critic. Study of Tea Service by Aldo Rossi.

COMPOSITION AND LAYOUT

Composition with focus on a central area. The compositional approach embraces sequence of frames and layers of individual elements (wiper, outline of a car, etc.) at varying scale to emphasize the rendered view. Perspective. View through windshield. Spray paint on ink line drawing on 30" x 40" mylar.
Ronn W. Yong (Student), Kent State University. C. Graves Jr., C. Harker, and T. Stauffer, Studio Critics. Corporate Headquarters for Sherwin & Williams, Cleveland, Ohio.

DRAWINGS COMBINED IN ONE COMPOSITION

This section illustrates examples of projects that combine more than one drawing into one composition.

CONSIDERATIONS TO COMBINE DRAWINGS IN ONE COMPOSITION

A good layout requires a good design scheme. To combine drawings in one composite presentation, the following points are important considerations:

• Composition based on the relationships among the drawings
• Attention to primary and secondary drawings
• Determination of hierarchy to reinforce emphasis and clarity
• Confirmation of the substance of design content
• Creation of the degree of abstraction
• Selection of the graphic techniques

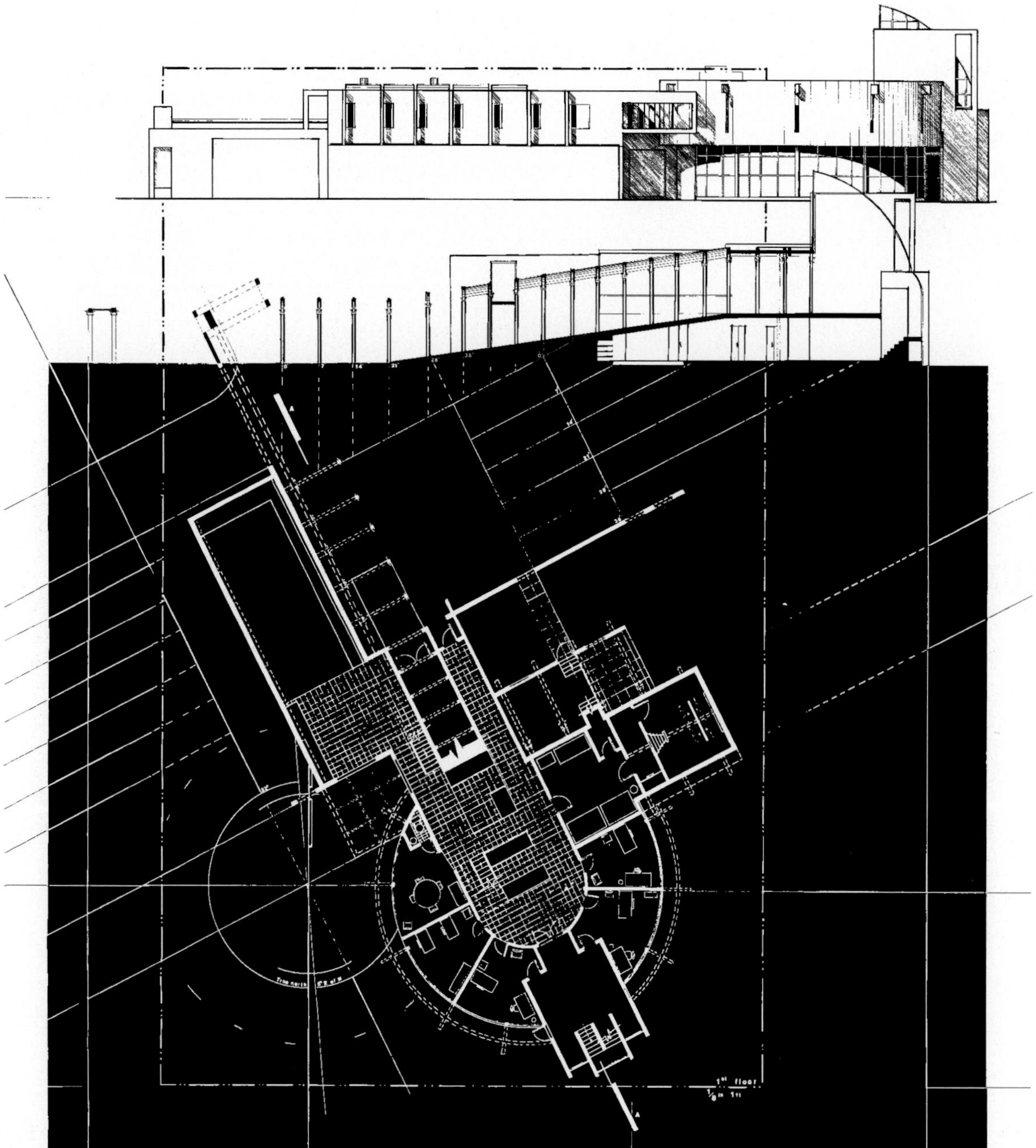

DRAWINGS COMBINED IN ONE COMPOSITION

POSITIVE-NEGATIVE

The composition engages positive and negative images of orthographic drawings. The reverse image of the floor plan creates a base line for the section drawing above. Elevation, section and floor plan. Ink on vellum positive-negative drawings. (This project required the use of reprographic techniques for the final presentation boards as an aid in the understanding of operations of blueprint facilities.)

Kevin Schellenbach (Student)
Savannah College of Art and Design
M. Saleh Uddin, Studio Critic
Savannah Blueprint and Reprographics

DRAWINGS COMBINED IN ONE COMPOSITION

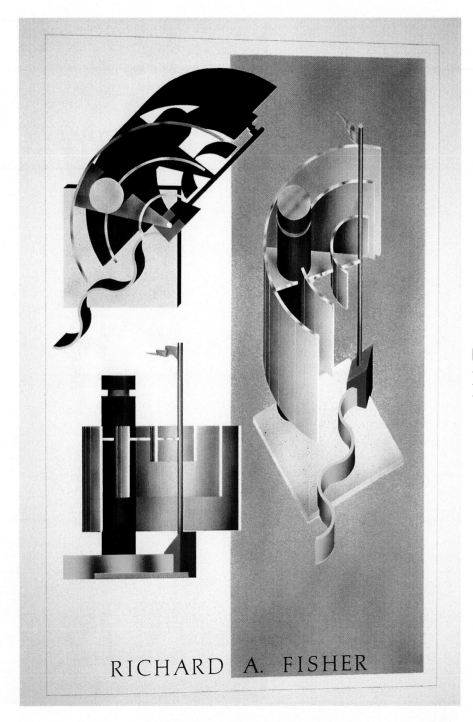

BACKGROUND

The background created for the axonometric drawing unifies all three drawings (roof plan, elevation and axonometric) in one composition. Use of frame and formal lettering further accentuate the completeness of the composition.

Richard A. Fisher (Student)
Savannah College of Art and Design. M. Saleh Uddin, Studio Critic.

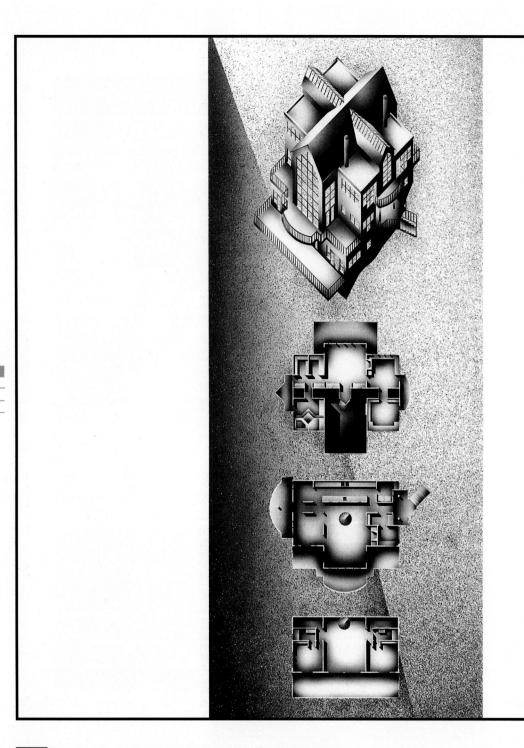

DRAWINGS COMBINED IN ONE COMPOSITION

FIGURE-GROUND

The vertical figure-ground composition of the drawing emphasizes the simple vertical form of the building. Axonometric and floor plans. Airbrush using acrylic inks on cold press illustration board.

House+House Architects, California
Mark English, Renderer
Green Residence, Woodside, California

DRAWINGS COMBINED IN ONE COMPOSITION

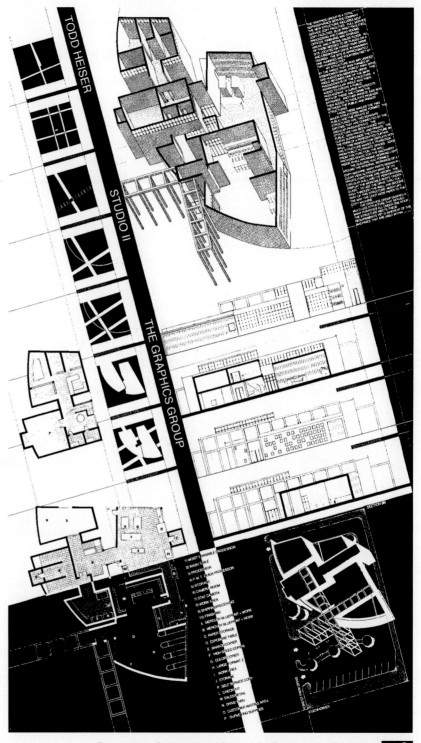

DIAGONAL EMPHASIS

Composition with diagonal emphasis. The presentation uses a diagonal format that refers to the relationship between the new site and the present site of the existing facilities in the historic district of Savannah (grid pattern). The presentation is composed of the schematic diagrams on its form-evolution, the site plan, floor plans, elevations, sections, plan-obliques and descriptive text. Ink on vellum positive-negative drawings.

Todd Heiser (Student)
Savannah College of Art and Design. M. Saleh Uddin, Studio Critic
Savannah Blueprint and Reprographics

DRAWINGS COMBINED IN ONE COMPOSITION

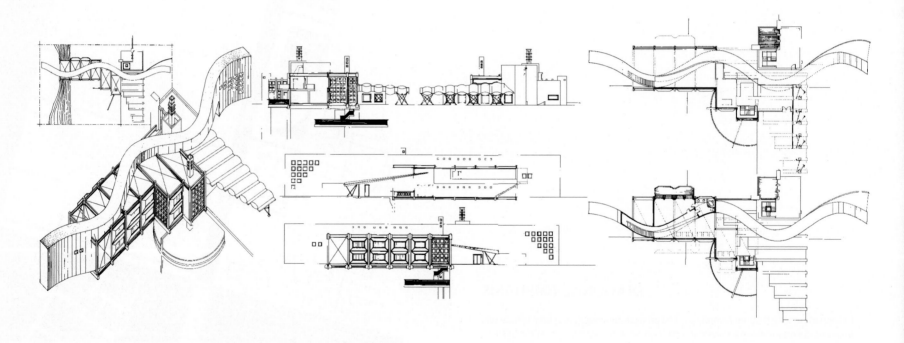

WITHOUT BACKGROUND OR FRAME

Various types of drawings combined in one drawing sheet. Strong curvilinear forms in plans and axonometric at both ends emphasize the rectilinear elevation and section drawings in the middle (no background or frame). Site plan, floor plans, sections, elevations and axonometric. Ink on mylar.

John Crump (Student), Savannah College of Art and Design. M. Saleh Uddin, Studio Critic. Dwelling with a Bridge.

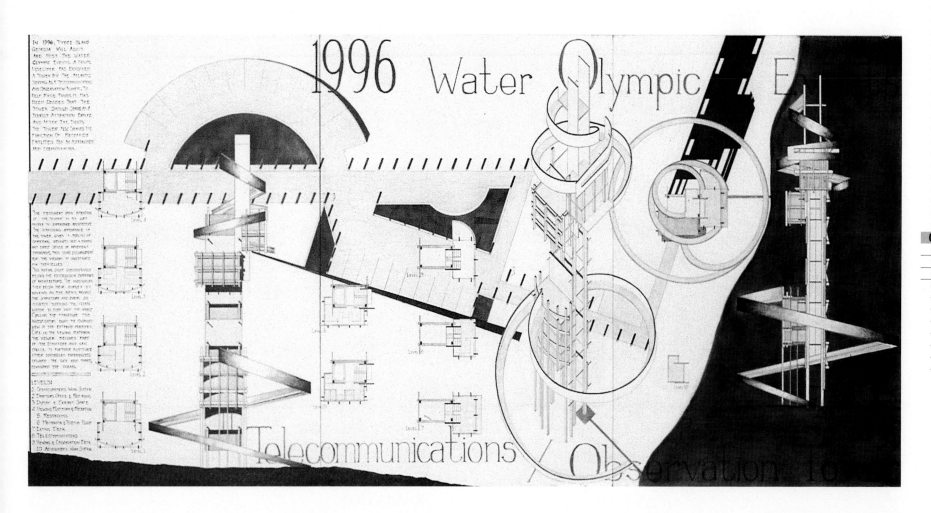

SCALE VARIATION

The composition of site plan, floor plans, elevations, and axonometric engages a wide range of scale and drawing types in one drawing. Site plan drawing spread over the presentation board creates the background for all other drawings, including a negative elevation insert on the water. Lead pencil on illustration board.

Catherine Ashton (Student), Savannah College of Art and Design. M. Saleh Uddin, Studio Critic. Lighthouse and Telecommunications Tower.

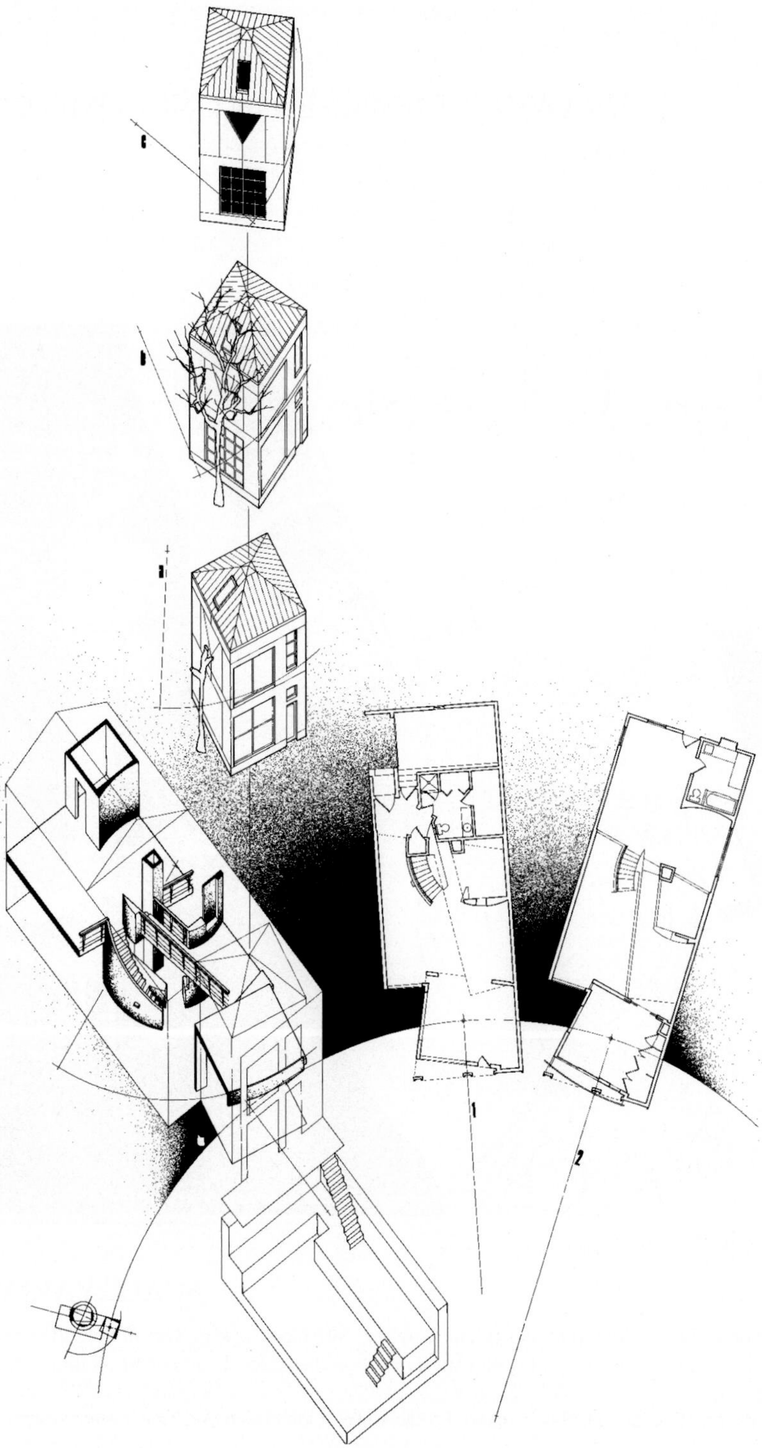

DRAWINGS COMBINED IN ONE COMPOSITION

RADIATION

Composition using segmental radiation. Exploded axonometric and plan composite. India ink on mylar.
House+House Architects, California
Michael Baushke, Renderer
Chason Residence, San Francisco, California

DRAWINGS COMBINED IN
ONE COMPOSITION

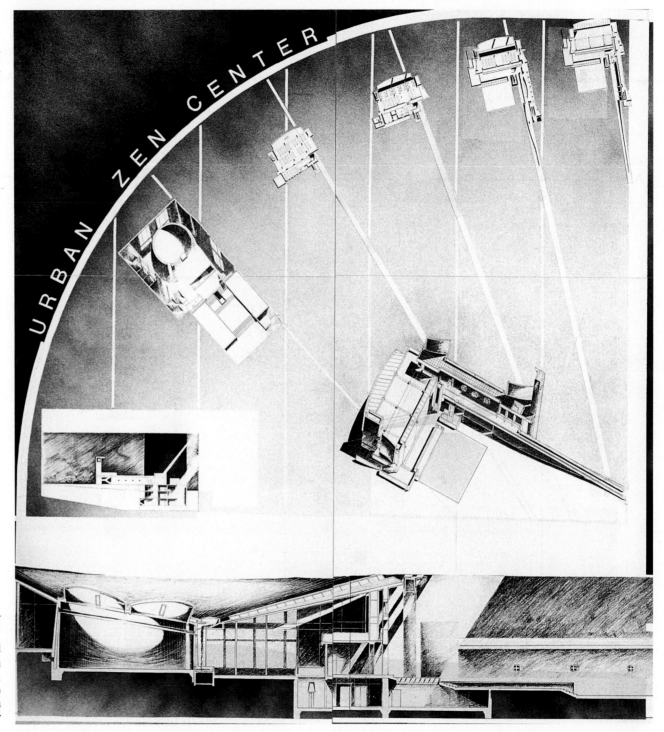

URBAN ZEN CENTER

RADIATION

Composition using segmental radiation. Ink and
pencil drawings arranged on textured paper with
airbrush gradation in black.
Liao Kok Chuan (Student)
University of Southwestern Louisiana
George Loli, Studio Critic. Urban Zen Center

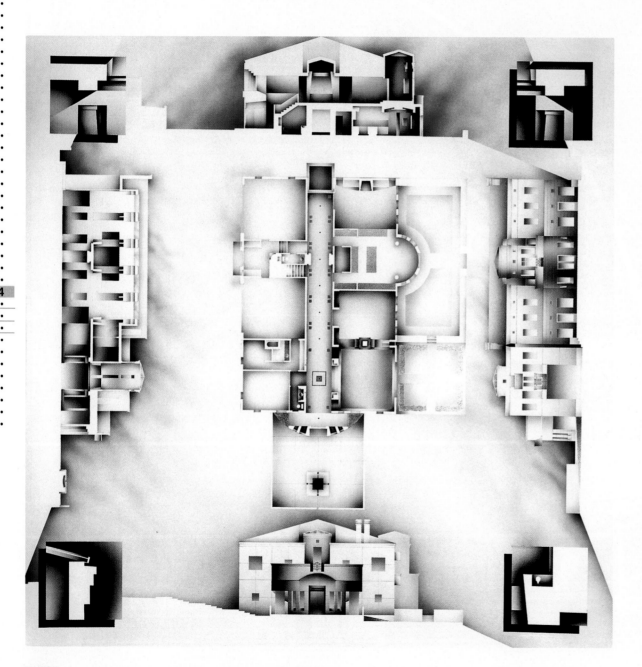

074

REFERENTIAL

The overall composition emphasizes the importance of each of the four cardinal directions in the design concept and is statically balanced to reflect harmony. Fold-out plan, section and elevation. Airbrush using acrylic inks on cold press illustration board.

House+House Architects, California
Mark English, Renderer
Liu Residence, Hillsborough, California

DRAWINGS COMBINED IN ONE COMPOSITION

THE SAVANNAH COLLEGE
OF ART AND DESIGN

ENTRY-PATH-PLACE

The Entry-Path-Place exercise was a free spatial expression of an architectural space form function problem. The goals were definition, articulation, investigation, and experimentation with the basic elements of architecture: entry, Path or passage and Place. The basic design elements of Point, Line, Plane and Volume were expanded upon to create a formal vocabulary. For the general composition the students were to consider the use of active structural grids, systems of geometry, the dynamics of asymmetry, the linear-curvilinear and solid-void contrasts.

Student name:

Johnathan Biron
Frederic Amey

Studio I Fall 1989
Instructor: Mohammed Uddin

GRIDS

Grids combine these two projects into one composition. Three-dimensional axonometric drawings arranged diagonally to counter-balance heavily rendered (shadow) plan drawings. Site plan, floor plan and axonometric. Ink, color pencil and adhesive color film on mylar.

Johnathan Biron and Frederic Amey (Students)
Savannah College of Art and Design. M. Saleh Uddin, Studio Critic
Entry-Path-Place

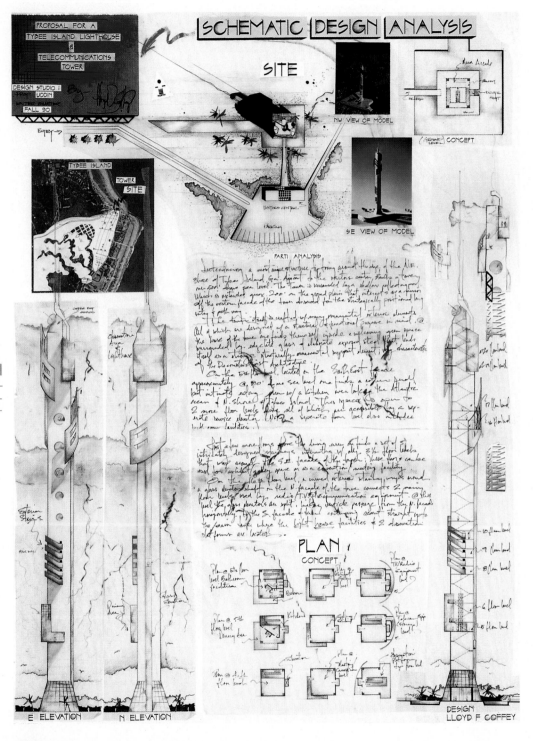

DRAWINGS COMBINED IN ONE COMPOSITION

USE OF GRAPHICS

Schematic design presentation combines yellow tracing paper drawings, site photograph and model photograph. Prismacolor pencil shades (clouds) and freehand text effectively unify all torn paper drawings and photographs into one composition.

Lloyd Coffey (Student), Savannah College of Art and Design. M. Saleh Uddin, Studio Critic. Tybee Island Lighthouse and Telecommunications Tower.

DRAWINGS COMBINED IN ONE COMPOSITION

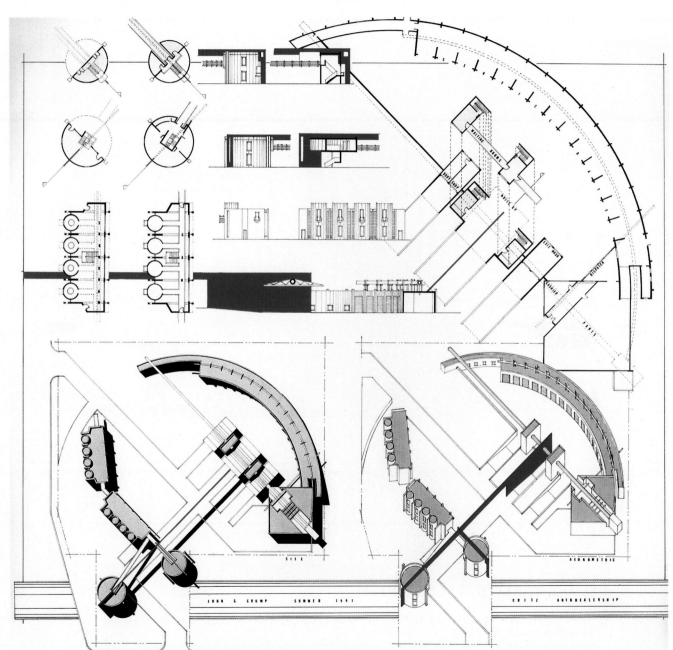

DESIGN ELEMENT

Composition uses dominant semi-circular sunken plan form to organize all other drawings in the total presentation. Dot screen and color adhesive film on ink on mylar drawing.

John Crump (Student)
Savannah College of Art and Design
M. Saleh Uddin, Studio Critic
Critz Auto Dealership (BMW-GM)

DRAWINGS COMBINED IN ONE COMPOSITION

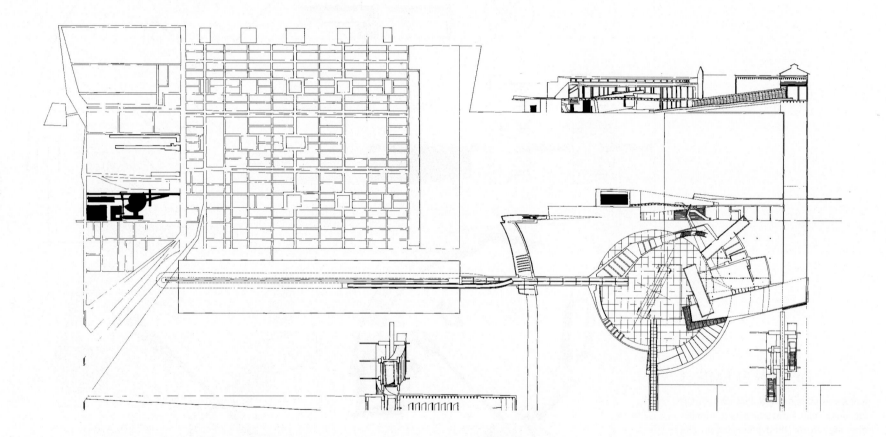

SCALE VARIATION/REFERENTIAL

Various types of drawings (at different scale) combined in a single composition by extending referential lines from one drawing to the other. Site plan within the city grid, floor plan section and elevation.
Kevin Rose (Student), Savannah College of Art and Design. Fernando Munilla and Robert Vuyosevich, Studio Critics.

DRAWINGS COMBINED IN ONE COMPOSITION

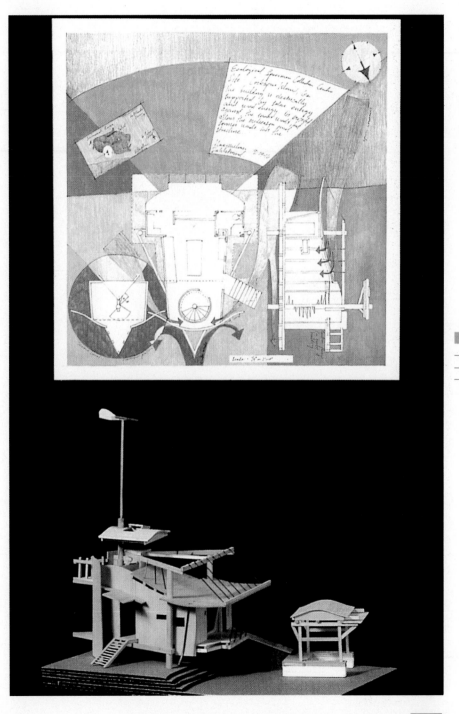

PHOTOGRAPHIC TECHNIQUE

Prismacolor pencil on ink line drawing and balsa wood model, photographed together using a black background to combine two-dimensional drawing and three-dimensional model in one presentation.

Maximilian Dahlstrand (Student), Savannah College of Art and Design. Deirdre Hardy, Studio Critic. Marine Specimen Collection Station.

COMPOSITE MONTAGE

COMPOSITE MONTAGE

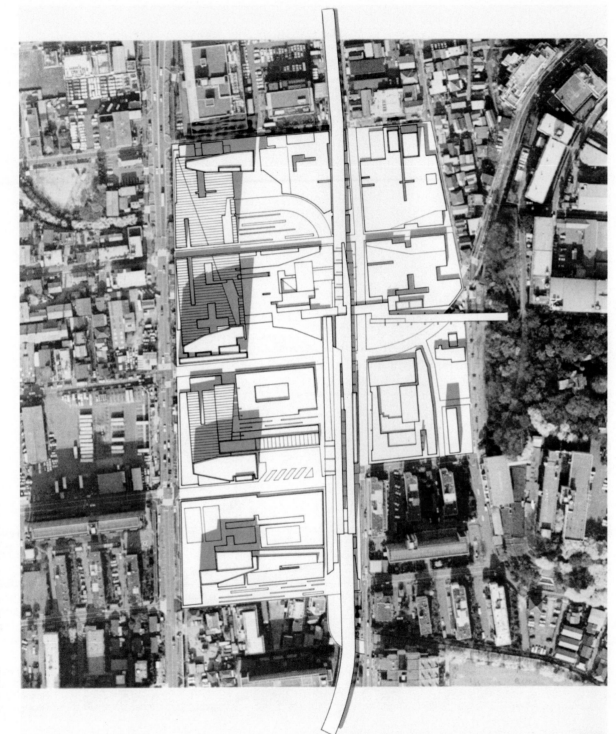

PHOTOMONTAGE
Aerial Photograph + Site Plan Drawing

Aerial composite plan. A print from ink on mylar originals is directly collaged with the aerial plan (photograph). Adhesive screen tone is then applied to indicate the limits of shadows. This drawing is made to study the insertion of a new industrial arts precinct within the existing city fabric. It describes the main artery of transportation, the siting of the taller masses of the office towers, a new park (shown striped) and the connection to an existing park (to the right).

Franklin D. Israel Design Associates, California
Drawing by George Yu and Jay Deguchi
Bunka Shutter and the New Industrial City,
Tokyo, Japan

COMPOSITE MONTAGE

PHOTOMONTAGE
Aerial Photograph + Site Plan Drawing

Aerial photograph photocopied on 22" x 30" vellum. Portions of the photocopied image were removed and the proposed site plan was redrawn in graphite. The layered character of the site is emphasized by the building of an artificial ground plane suspended over the roadway and river.

Academic project. University of Colorado, Denver, Colorado
Student: E. J. Mead. Studio Critic: Douglas Darden
School for the Teaching of Building Trades
Riverbank Park, New Jersey

COMPOSITE MONTAGE

PHOTOMONTAGE
Model Photograph + Floor Plan

Black-and-white model photograph superimposed on reverse (negative) ink drawing.

Mehrdad Yazdani, California
Overland House, Los Angeles, California

COMPOSITE MONTAGE

084

PHOTOMONTAGE
Photograph + Exploded Perspective

Ink on mylar perspective of the architectural components superimposed on the photograph of the skies over the Bikini Islands.
Frank Lupo, Lupo/Rowen Architects, New York. Perry Rubenstein Gallery.

COMPOSITE MONTAGE

PHOTOMONTAGE
Aerial Site Photograph + Rendering of New Proposal

The site photograph shows the limited space between the ferry terminals and the city. The scale and extent of the design was first mapped out and sketched on tracing paper over the aerial site photograph. The line drawing was then transferred onto the photographic print and rendered with airbrush using acrylic paint and gouache. The intention of this finished photomontage was to propose a design scheme that creates a public piazza by relocating the ferry terminals.

Greg-Scott-Young / EMTB Architects, Australia
Peter Edgeley, Renderer, Australia
Piazza and Ferry Terminal near Sydney Opera House, Sydney, Australia

Preliminary sketch overlaid on existing site photograph.

Existing site photograph.

Proposal rendered directly on photographic print.

COMPOSITE MONTAGE

PHOTOMONTAGE
Photograph + Rendering of Proposed Building

The site boundaries were identified first. The essential geometry of the view was analyzed, i.e., vanishing points and horizon line. The tower was then plotted on tracing paper using the same camera position, height and center of view. The linework was then transferred onto the photographic print using a chinagraph pencil and the glazing areas were airbrushed in. Finally, using a mixed media of acrylic and gouache, the structure was rendered over the top. The drawing is made to show the insertion of a new tower within the existing city fabric.

Daryl Jackson Architects, Australia
Peter Edgeley, Renderer, Australia
Office Tower, 120 Collins St., Melbourne, Australia

Site photograph with boundaries identified.

EYE LINE

VANISHING POINT

COMPOSITE MONTAGE

PHOTOMONTAGE
Site Photograph +
Model Photograph

The photo collage combines a black-and-white image of a typical nitty-gritty New York City midtown corner with a black-and-white photo of a very detailed half-inch scale model of a prototype. The model was lit and shot from the same angle as the site photo and carefully cut in. The combined photos were then reshot and partially hand-tinted with colored photographic dyes. The elements of the design for this newsstand are based on the abstraction of the parts of a printing press. The design places the newsstand among the sidewalk iconography of fire hydrants, street lights and mailboxes.

Frederic Schwartz
Anderson/Schwartz Architects, New York
with Chris Calori and
David Vanden-Eynden.
Hand-tinting by Karen Maloof
New York City Newsstand Competition,
New York, New York, 1990

COMPOSITE MONTAGE

Existing site photograph

PHOTOMONTAGE
Site Photograph +
Model Photograph

Electronic photomontage. Model photograph scanned into site photograph to show proposed building in the surrounding context. Perspective calculated and 1/8" model photographed to match vanishing points. Montaged in ColorStudio on Macintosh; output on photographic film.

Harlan Hambright/InSite, Georgia
Herald Square, Washington, D.C.

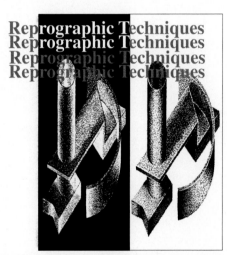

Reprographic Techniques
Reprographic Techniques
Reprographic Techniques
Reprographic Techniques

Reprographic Techniques ■

Basic Reproduction Means
Reverse Technique
Color Reproduction and Color Photocopy

BASIC REPRODUCTION MEANS
REVERSE TECHNIQUE

BASIC REPRODUCTION MEANS

Reproduction of black-and-white drawings may be broadly divided into the following categories:

1. Diazo Process (Ammonia Print)
2. Xerographic/Electrostatic/Digital Plain Paper Copy Process
3. Pressure Diazo Process (No Ammonia)
4. Photo Process using Silver Emulsion (Darkroom)
5. Photo Mechanical Transfer (PMT/STAT)
6. Negative Positive Reversal

1. DIAZO PROCESS

Diazo process (ammonia) involves copying on a special paper with yellow dye. The original drawing has to be transparent or translucent, so that the light can pass through to expose the copy paper. The more light (exposure) the copy paper gets, the lighter the print becomes. Less light will create a darker print. Diazo process is capable of producing the following variety of reproductions (compare examples).

• Blueline Print (Opaque Paper)
• Blackline Print (Opaque Paper)
• Sepia (Brownline, Transluscent Paper)
• Erasable Sepia (Paper)
• Film Sepia (Black or Brown Erasable Mylar)
• Diazochrome (Clear/Transparent-1 Color)

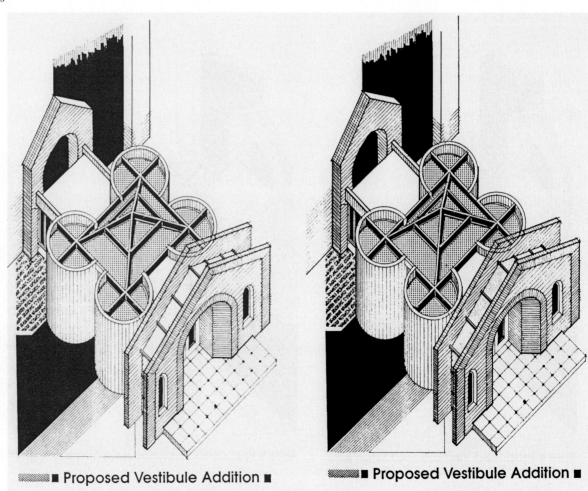

Diazo Process: Blueline (Opaque)　　Diazo Process: Blackline (Opaque)

Drawing: M. S. Uddin.　Diazo Print Courtesy: C&D Repro/Graphics Inc., Baton Rouge, Louisiana

■ **Proposed Vestibule Addition** ■　■ **Proposed Vestibule Addition** ■

091

BASIC REPRODUCTION MEANS

Proposed Vestibule Addition

Diazo Process: Sepia

Proposed Vestibule Addition

Diazo Process: Erasable Sepia

Proposed Vestibule Addition

Diazo Process: Film Sepia

BASIC REPRODUCTION MEANS

■ Proposed Vestibule Addition ■

Diazo Process: Diazochrome (Transparent/Blue)

■ Proposed Vestibule Addition ■

Diazo Process: Diazochrome (Transparent/Black)

2. XEROGRAPHIC / ELECTROSTATIC / DIGITAL PLAIN PAPER COPY PROCESS

Basically large format photocopy process capable of copying on a roll of bond paper. These machines usually print up to 36" of width and 50' of length. The length varies from machine to machine.

• Copies on bond paper, vellum, and mylar
• Enlarges, reduces: 25% to 200%
• Advanced machines are capable of making prints in negative and mirror image.
• Advanced machines have the option to link with a computer to scan images and store in a disk. Drawings may be viewed and corrected before making prints. Pen width of CAD drawings may be changed before printing.

3. PRESSURE DIAZO PROCESS

Uses activator chemical, without any ammonia. Appropriate for small offices.

4. PHOTO PROCESS

Darkroom process involving silver emulsion and large-format camera on track.

• More permanent and archival quality reproduction
• Accurate and wide range of enlargement and reduction
• Original may be as big as 48" x 96", depending on the size of the copy or vacuum board
• Reproduces on film negative or positive (line, screen and tone)
• Prints on photo paper and film mylar

5. PHOTO MECHANICAL TRANSFER (PMT/STAT)

Direct photographic transfer (positive) without intermediate negative.

REVERSE (NEGATIVE) TECHNIQUE

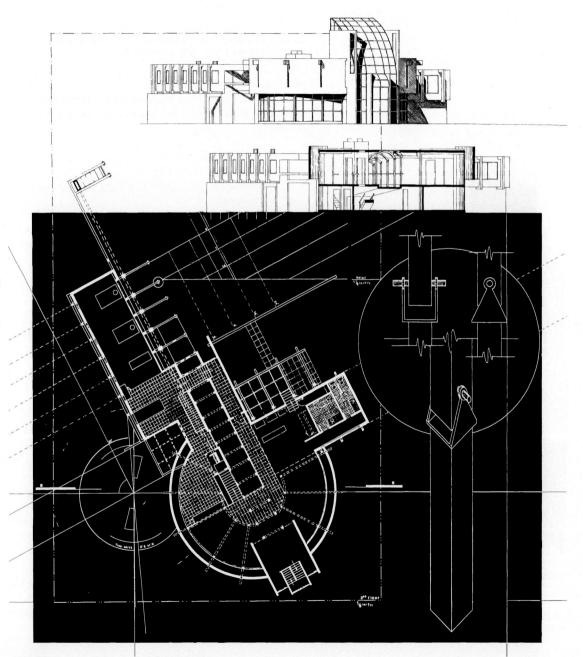

NEGATIVE-POSITIVE REVERSAL

Advanced blackline copy machines (as well as color laser copy machines) are capable of producing negative copies as well as mirror images of a regular blackline drawing. Negative copies produce white line drawing on black background which may be effectively used to emphasize certain part(s) of the drawing or to compose the overall image. This image is reproduced using two simple reprographic steps. First a negative copy of the desired drawing was created in a color laser copy machine. Since color copy machines can take only 11"x17" originals, the drawing was copied in several pieces and pasted together on large white bond paper. Black marker and technical pen were used to create a larger background and retouch details. The final copy was made on a large blackline copy machine on white vellum. Final size 30"x40".

Kevin Schellenbach (Student)
Savannah College of Art and Design
M. Saleh Uddin, Studio Critic
Savannah Blueprint and Reprographics

COLOR REPRODUCTION AND COLOR PHOTOCOPY

COLOR REPRODUCTION AND COLOR PHOTOCOPY

1

2

3

4

COLOR REPRODUCTION MEANS

Reproduction of color drawing may be achieved through various means, depending on the size of the drawing and purpose of the reproduction. For example if the drawing has to be projected on a screen for a large audience, 35mm slide format would be the appropriate means of reproduction. But if the drawing is to be documented for a personal portfolio and the original drawing is 11"x17" or smaller, color laser photocopy would be the effective means of reproduction.

Color reproduction means may be broadly devided into these two categories:

• Color Laser Photocopy (Electrostatic/Plain Paper) Process
• Color Photographic (Darkroom) Process

Color photographic process includes the following means of reproduction:

• Color Photo Print from 35mm Color Film Negative
• Color Photo Print from Medium Format Film Negative
  (varies from 1-3/4" x 1-3/4" to 2-1/4" x 6-11/16" but traditional format is 2-1/4" x 2-1/4")
• Color Photo Print from 4" x 5" Film Negative
• Color PMT (Photo Mechanical Transfer)
• Color Slide (Film Positive or Transparency), 35mm
• Color Slide (Film Positive or Transparency), 4"x 5" and other formats

1. Color Film Negative
2. 35mm Slide (Film Positive)
3. Medium Format Slide 1-3/4" x 2-1/4"
4. 4" x 5" Slide (Film Positive or Transparency)

COLOR LASER COPIER

Besides copying color images a color laser copy machine can be used for other reprographic purposes. These include:
• Color Copy on Transparencies for Overhead Projection
• Color Copy from Regular 35mm Film Negative or Film Positive (Slide)
• Image Editing: Framing, Blanking, Image Segmentation, Shift Image,
  Mirror Image, Image Composition, Color Registration

Some of the useful features that may be explored for reproduction of architectural drawings are illustrated below:

• Negative-Positive Reversal
• Background Creation
• Color Creation (from Black-and-White Original)
• Color Conversion & Negative-Positive Reversal
  (Single Color from Full Color Original)
• Color Conversion (Solarization from Monochrome Original)
• Color Conversion (Single Color from Monochrome Original)
• Enlargement and Reduction on Independent Horizontal-Vertical Axis

097

NEGATIVE-POSITIVE REVERSAL
Black and White
(Using Color Laser Photocopier)

Color laser copiers with reversal (negative) features allow copies to be made in negative as well as in mirror image. Negative copies produce white lines/dots on black background which may be used to emphasize certain moods or effects.

Adhesive dot screen on pen and ink sketch perspective.
M. Saleh Uddin
Project for an Urban Design Proposal

COLOR REPRODUCTION AND COLOR PHOTOCOPY

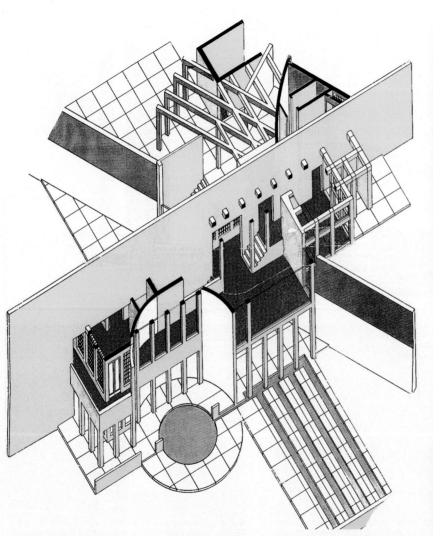
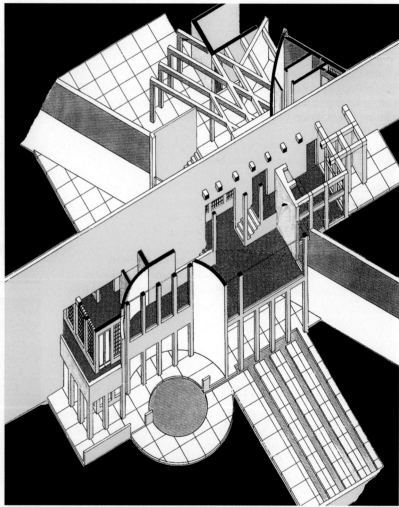

BACKGROUND CREATION (Using Color Laser Photocopier)

Most color copy machines are capable of creating a black background when the drawing is cut around the edges and the intended background area is exposed as a void area (no paper backing). These two color copies were made from the same original that was cut around the profile of the drawing. The left image was copied with white paper on the back of the drawing. The right image was copied without any white background. All cut areas (exposed to light) outside the drawing area created a black background.

John Biron (Student), Savannah College of Art and Design. M. Saleh Uddin, Studio Critic. House Chang(ed).

COLOR CREATION
from Black-and-White Original

(Using Color
Laser Photocopier)

Most color copy machines are capable of creating and converting color from a drawing.

• In the standard full-color mode an original is usually copied in full four color (cyan, magenta, yellow and black).

• Color may be added on a black-and-white image using single-color mode that creates a copy from cyan, magenta, yellow, black, blue, green, or red.

Ron C. Mathis (Student)
Southern University
M. Saleh Uddin, Studio Critic

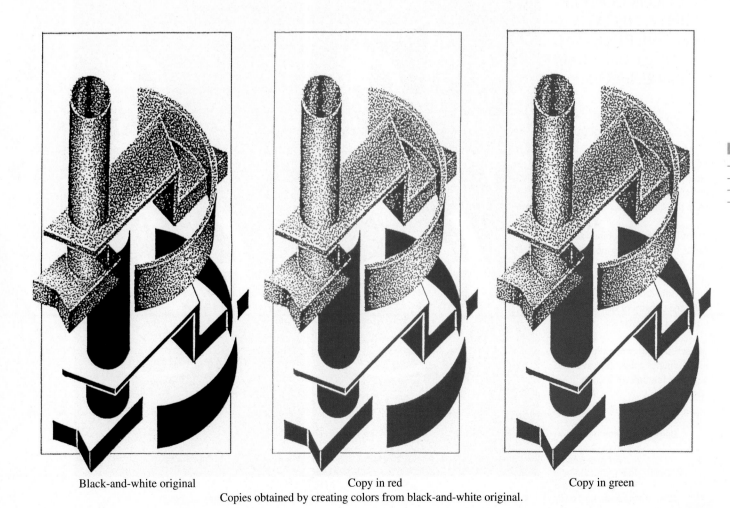

Black-and-white original   Copy in red   Copy in green
Copies obtained by creating colors from black-and-white original.

COLOR REPRODUCTION AND COLOR PHOTOCOPY

COLOR CONVERSION & NEGATIVE-POSITIVE REVERSAL
Single Color from Full-Color Original

(Using Color Laser Photocopier)

• Colors may be changed into different colors for a total image or designated areas of the image that have the same color.

Color laser copy machines are capable of reproducing negative as well as mirror images in a single color irrespective of the color of the original drawing. In a negative copy the density of the original is reproduced in reverse.

These images were reproduced using single color, positive and negative features in a color laser copy machine.

Catherine Ashton (Student)
Savannah College of
Art and Design
M. Saleh Uddin, Studio Critic
Lighthouse and
Telecommunications Tower

Original full color model photograph

Copy in green

Reverse (negative) in green

COLOR CONVERSION
Solarization from
Monochrome Original
(Using Color
Laser Photocopier)

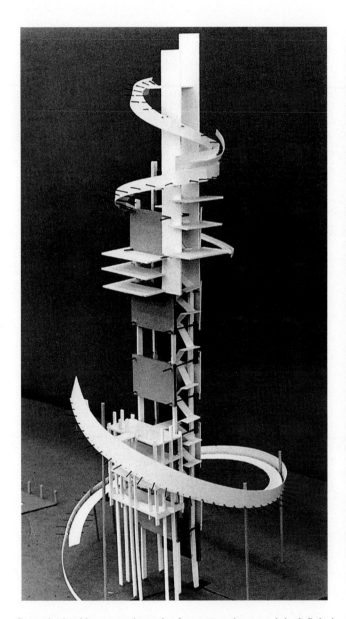

101

Surprising results may be achieved by converting, and altering colors. By rearranging or altering the colors of a monochrome photograph original, solarized images and other effects may be created.

• Colors may be changed for a total image or designated areas of the image that have the same color into a different color.

Catherine Ashton (Student)
Savannah College of Art and Design
M. Saleh Uddin, Studio Critic
Lighthouse and
Telecommunications Tower

Copy obtained by converting color from monochrome original. Solarized effect achieved by designating green color for a particular gray shade.

COLOR REPRODUCTION AND COLOR PHOTOCOPY

  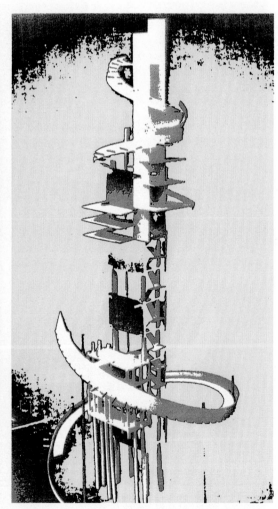

Copies obtained by converting color from monochrome original. Resulting copy of the monochrome photo used as an original and copied again using color conversion mode to create these solarized images.

Catherine Ashton (Student), Savannah College of Art and Design. M. Saleh Uddin, Studio Critic. Lighthouse and Telecommunications Tower.

COLOR CREATION/
CONVERSION
Single Color from
Monochrome Original

(Using Color Laser
Photocopier)

Specific portion(s) of a black-and-white original with the same tonal value may be produced in a single color by designating a color for that value.

The image is produced by designating the dark black area of the original to copy in cyan.

Kevin Schellenbach (Student)
Savannah College of
Art and Design
M. Saleh Uddin, Studio Critic
Savannah Blueprint
and Reprographics

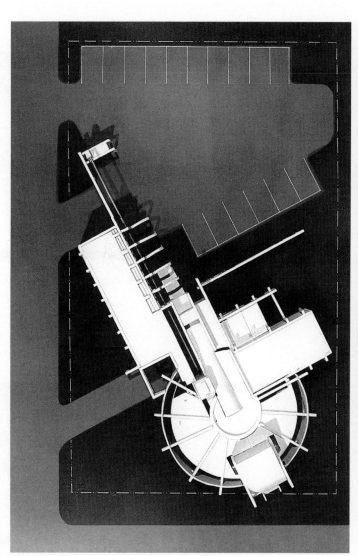

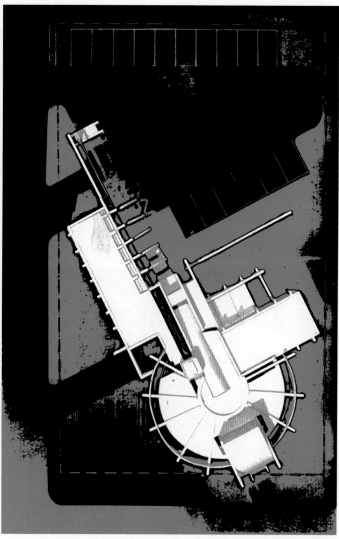

Original black-and-white model photograph

Copy obtained by converting dark black areas into cyan.

COLOR REPRODUCTION AND COLOR PHOTOCOPY

ENLARGEMENT/REDUCTION ON INDEPENDENT HORI-ZONTAL-VERTICAL AXIS (Using Color Photocopier)

This feature allows the setting of ratios independently in vertical and/or horizontal directions in 1% increments. By doing this the image changes into a new shape.

Gary Coccoluto (Student), Savannah College of Art and Design.
M. Saleh Uddin, Studio Critic. Dwelling with a Bridge (Model Photograph).

Original image. Vertical ratio 100%, horizontal ratio 100%.

Copy obtained using bidirectional reduction/enlargement with a vertical ratio of 130% and a horizontal ratio of 80%.

Copy obtained using bidirectional reduction/enlargement with a vertical ratio of 80% and a horizontal ratio of 130%.

• Takefumi Aida (Japan) • Anthony Ames • Tadao Ando (Japan) •
Natalye Appel Architects • David Baker Associates • R. L. Binder
• Bryan Cantley + Kevin O'Donnell / Synesis • Stephen K. Chung
• Carlos Concepcion • Cor-Tex / Neil Denari • Douglas Darden •
Peter Edgeley (Australia)/Daryl Jackson • Ellerbe Becket • Richard
Ferrier • Hiromi Fujii (Japan) • Gilbert Gorski/Tate & Snyder
Architects • Jawaid Haider • Harlan Hambright/Khon Pederson Fox
Architects • Hariri & Hariri • HLW International • Steven Holl •
House+House • Franklin D. Israel • Helmut Jahn/Murphy/Jahn
Architects • Kajima Corporation (Japan) • Raymond Kappe •
Krueck & Sexton • Kisho Kurokawa (Japan) • David Leary & Laura
Owen • George Loli • Lubowicki/Lanier • Lupo/Rowen • Machado
and Silvetti • Mack Architects • David Mayernik • Morphosis • Eric
Owen Moss • Dean Nota • Pollari x Somol • Polshek and Partners
• Alexis Pontvik (Sweden) • Thomas Norman Rajkovich • Resolu-
tion:4 Architecture • Joyce Rosner/Sharon Tyler Architects •
Roth+Sheppard • Joel Sanders • Frederic Schwartz • Scogin Elam
and Bray • Kevin D. Scott • Smith-Miller+Hawkinson • Thomas
Sofranko • Shin Takamatsu (Japan) • Minoru Takeyama (Japan) •
Christine Tedesco • Tod Williams Billie Tsien • Bernard Tschumi
• M. Saleh Uddin • Riken Yamamoto + Field Shop (Japan) •
Mehrdad Yazdani • Ken Yeang (Malaysia) • Ronn Yong+Nicholas
Montan • Art Zendarski • 6+A Architects •

Composite • Professional Portfolio ■

106

Drawing: ▬
Hand-drawn in ink on Japanese paper. Drawing expressing the concept Yuragi-Fluctuation, and composition of spaces in the building with shading of each element of the wall.

Design: ▬
The architecture is composed of several parallel walls and posts, independent of functions created by them. There is no coherence between architectural elements and their functions. Between the relationship of these elements and each function a chaotic space is created. An observer may associate this chaotic space as an invisible space, a spatial effect of Yuragi-Fluctuation.

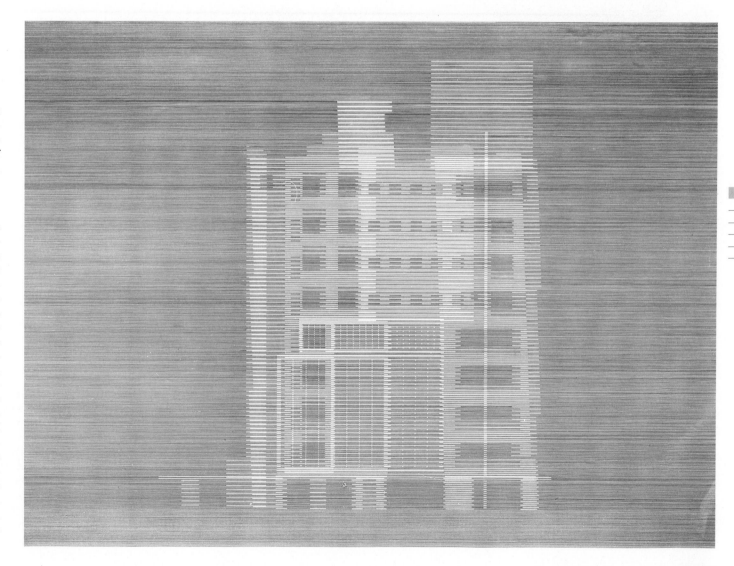

Drawing:
Hand-drawn with pencil on Japanese paper. Drawing showing the concept Yuragi - Fluctuation, and composition of spaces by layering of the walls.

Design:
The design intends to create a context different from the prevailing ambience, to suggest a new way in which the streetscape and the area in general could develop, and to provide the GKD Building with its own identity. In order to achieve this objective, multiple planar fragments, each endowed with a distinct image, are arranged in layers. This expresses the uneven and unstable process by which Japanese cities develop and provides an effective means of reinvigorating the area. Some planes are tilted and others are very orderly and independent. The *shoji*-like aluminum curtain wall and the huge aluminum lattice inserted among the planes are also distinct objects.

107

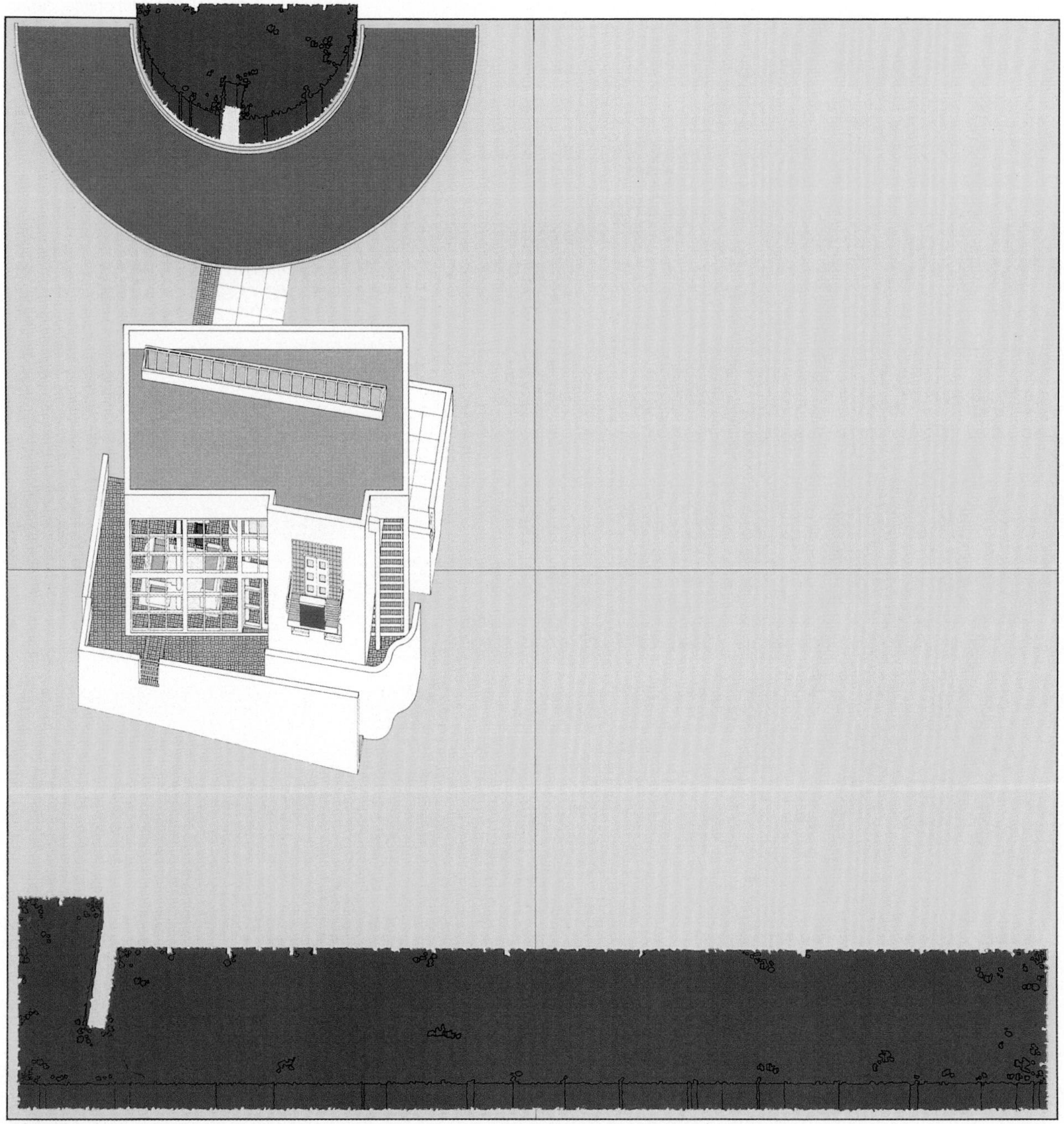

Anthony Ames Architect, Georgia ▬
House in Mississippi, Laurel, Mississippi

108

Drawing: ▬
Axonometric view composed with the site. Color adhesive film on pen-and-ink line drawing.

Design: ▬
Two rotated rectangles are superimposed so that the residual space created between the perimeters of each is treated as occupiable poche and contains the vertical circulation (stairs) and the service facilities. Spaces are arranged in two mutually diverse types establishing a dichotomy of both traditional, 'pre-modern' or discrete space—the concept of room (master bedroom and library) and modern space—overlapping, interpenetrating, and loosely defined spaces (living/dining areas and balconies).

Tadao Ando, Osaka, Japan
Theater on the Water, Tomamu, Hokkaido, Japan

Drawing:
Compositional site plan. Color pencil on drawing paper. 845mm x 1085mm.

Design:
A 6000-seat semicircular theater, northwest of the 'Church on the Water,'
designed to accommodate open-air concerts and fashion shows, and skating
events in winter. Set on a fan-shaped artificial pond, this amphitheater is
intersected by a long bridgelike stage and a freestanding colonade.

Tadao Ando, Osaka, Japan ━━━
Church on the Water, Tomamu, Hokkaido, Japan

━━ **Drawing:**
Transparent composite perspective. Line drawing in ink.

━━ **Design:**
Set within the scenic splendor of mountains in a cold northern region of Japan, this church is configured around a pond created by diverting a stream. The wall behind the altar is constructed entirely of glass, and can slide to the side, opening the chapel to receive the murmur of water, the fragrance of trees, and the song of birds. Here, people encounter nature directly.

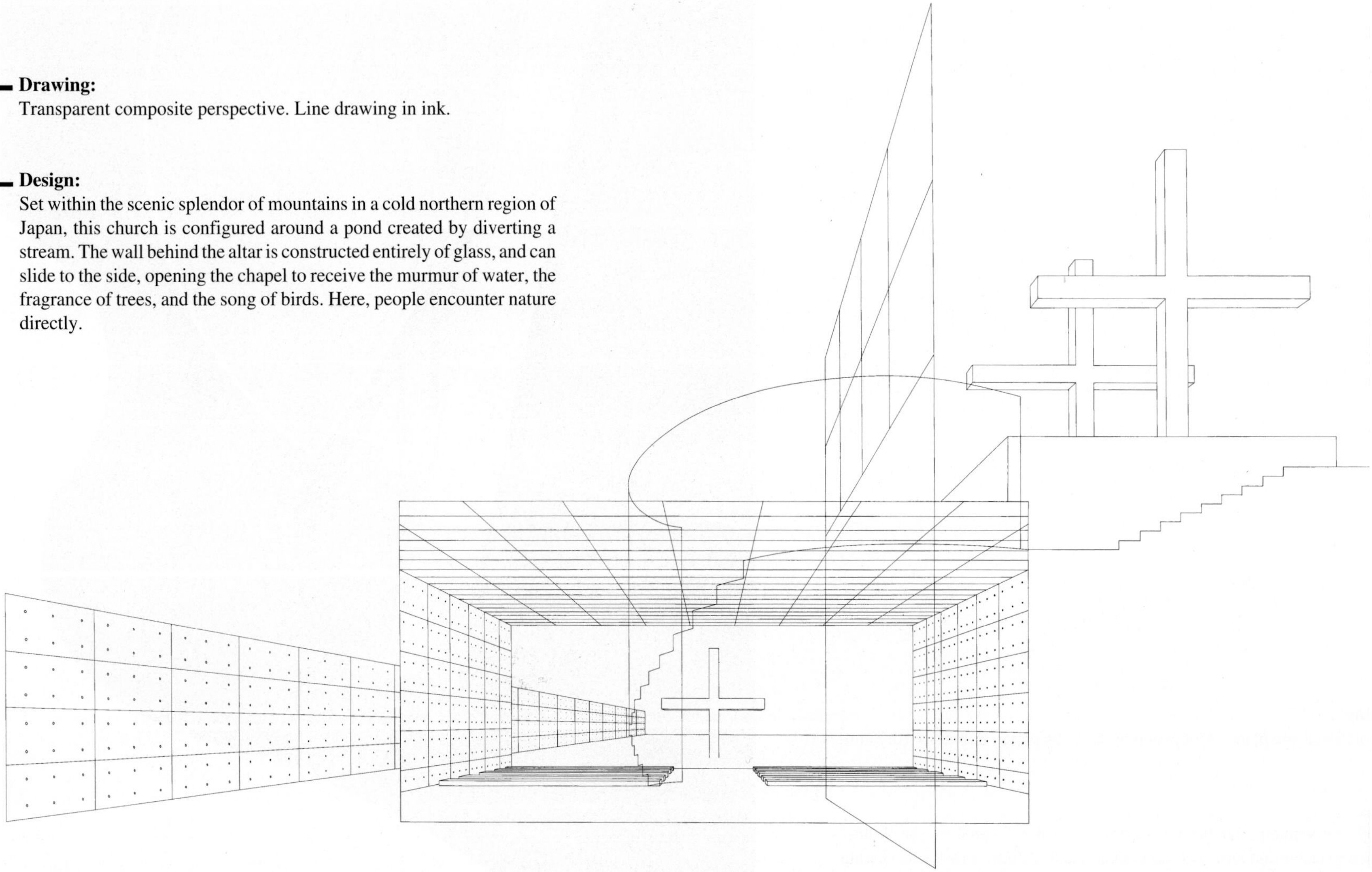

Natalye Appel Architects, Texas
Natalye Appel and Lee S. Olvera
Lightman Double-House, Houston, Texas

Drawing:

Combination of multiple orthographic projections. Site plan, elevations, and exploded axonometric view arranged at various scales. Ink and color film on 24"x24" illustration board.

Design:

An L-shaped building on the outer corner of the site, places the 3-story Main House/Gallery on the long leg of the 'L' while the Small House/Garage/Studio forms the shed-roofed short leg. At the intersection of the two wings is the covered third-floor roof deck, which gives the master suite a view of downtown Houston in the morning, and serves as the Grand Finale party spot at the end of each course. The corrugated Galvalume siding unites the two wings with a low-cost, durable material that relates to a nearby warehouse.

David Baker Associates Architects, California ━━
David Baker
Cafe Milano, Berkeley, California

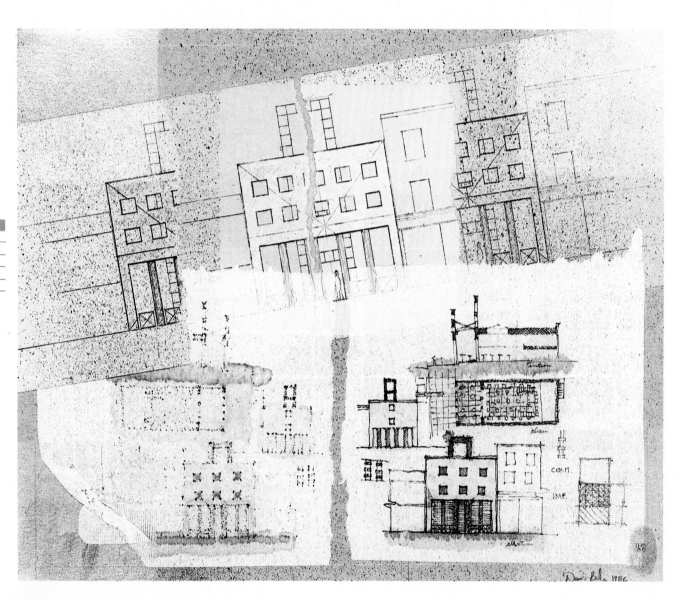

Drawing: ━
Collage. Mixed media. Line drawing photocopied on colored paper; ripped, reassembled, and rendered; ink sketches on paper napkin mounted to brown gator board.

Design: ━
Cafe Milano is a 3500 s.f. cafe in a renovated shoe store with new street facade, mezzanine structure, kitchen, and operable skylight.

David Baker Associates Architects, California
Nancy Whitcombe
Revenge of the Stuccoids House

Drawing:
Composite plans, sections, and elevations. Ink on
24"x36" vellum.

Design:
The stuccoids are modern gray stucco houses from the
flatlands which wage war with venerable hill houses
designed by Bernard Maybeck.

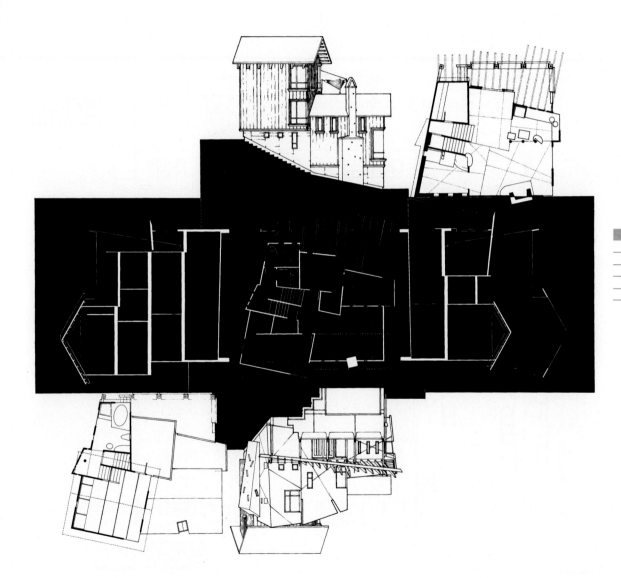

113

R. L. Binder, F.A.I.A. Architecture & Planning, California

LAUSD, Eagle Rock Elementary School, Eagle Rock, California

Chilin Huang, Drawing

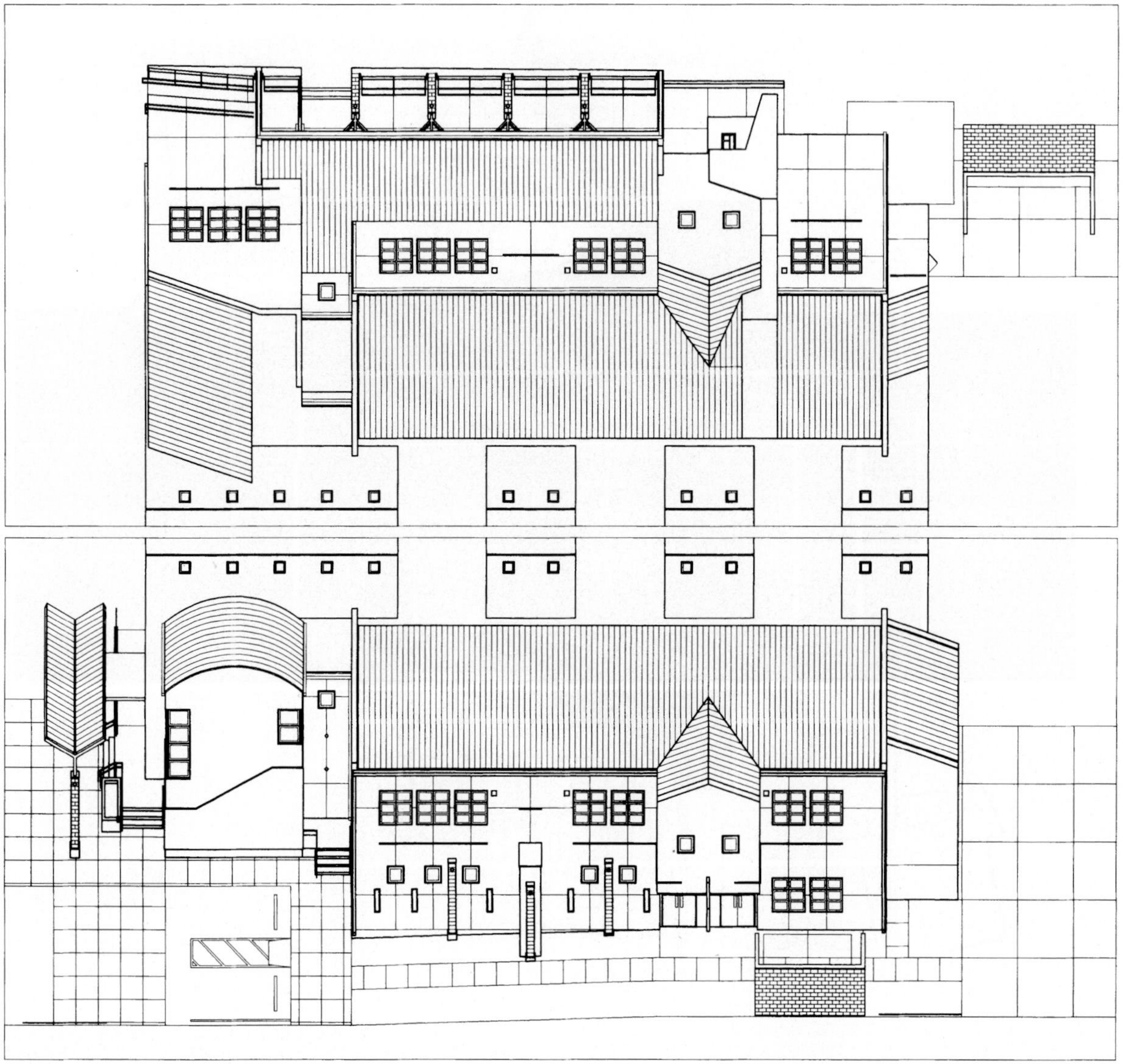

Drawing:

Composite elevations afford the ability to view both sides of the building simultaneously and to view the corresponding relationships between various parts otherwise hidden from each other. Drawn on AutoCAD Release 12.

Design:

The design of this magnet school was shaped in response to an existing 100-year-old elementary school campus. The stand-alone addition is referential in color and selected materials, while the form is compatible but independent.

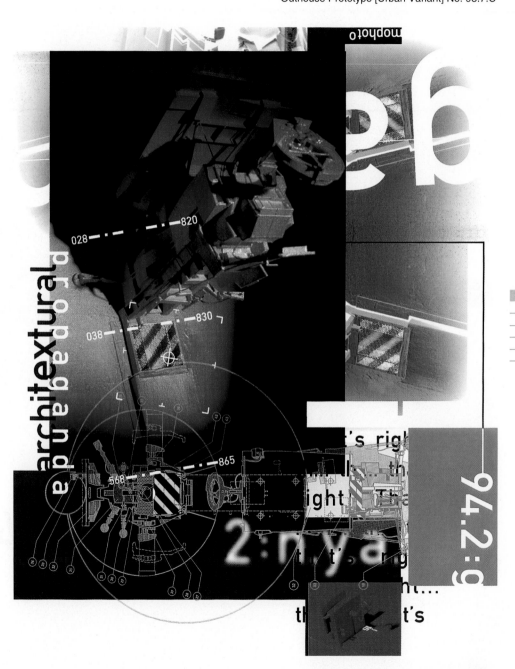

Drawing:

"Architextural" Composite. Visualization of kinetic, machine, indicator + targeting graphics, and deeply coded communication as an example of the synesis of the project. Full color electronic image integrating computer-manipulated, scanned, hand-drawn line work + images, orchestrated in QuarkXPress + Adobe Photoshop. 11" x 14" rainbow print.

Design:

A kinetic public restroom facility in response to the lack thereof, within the New York and Los Angeles communities. Outhouse deconstructs itself after each paid usage. A completely self-sustainable project, the pissoir incorporates moveable interior/exterior video programming + display. The ARCHITECTURE exists only when in use, otherwise the object becomes urban street sculpture.

Bryan Cantley + Kevin O'Donnell / Synesis
Outhouse Prototype [Urban Variant] No. 93.7:C

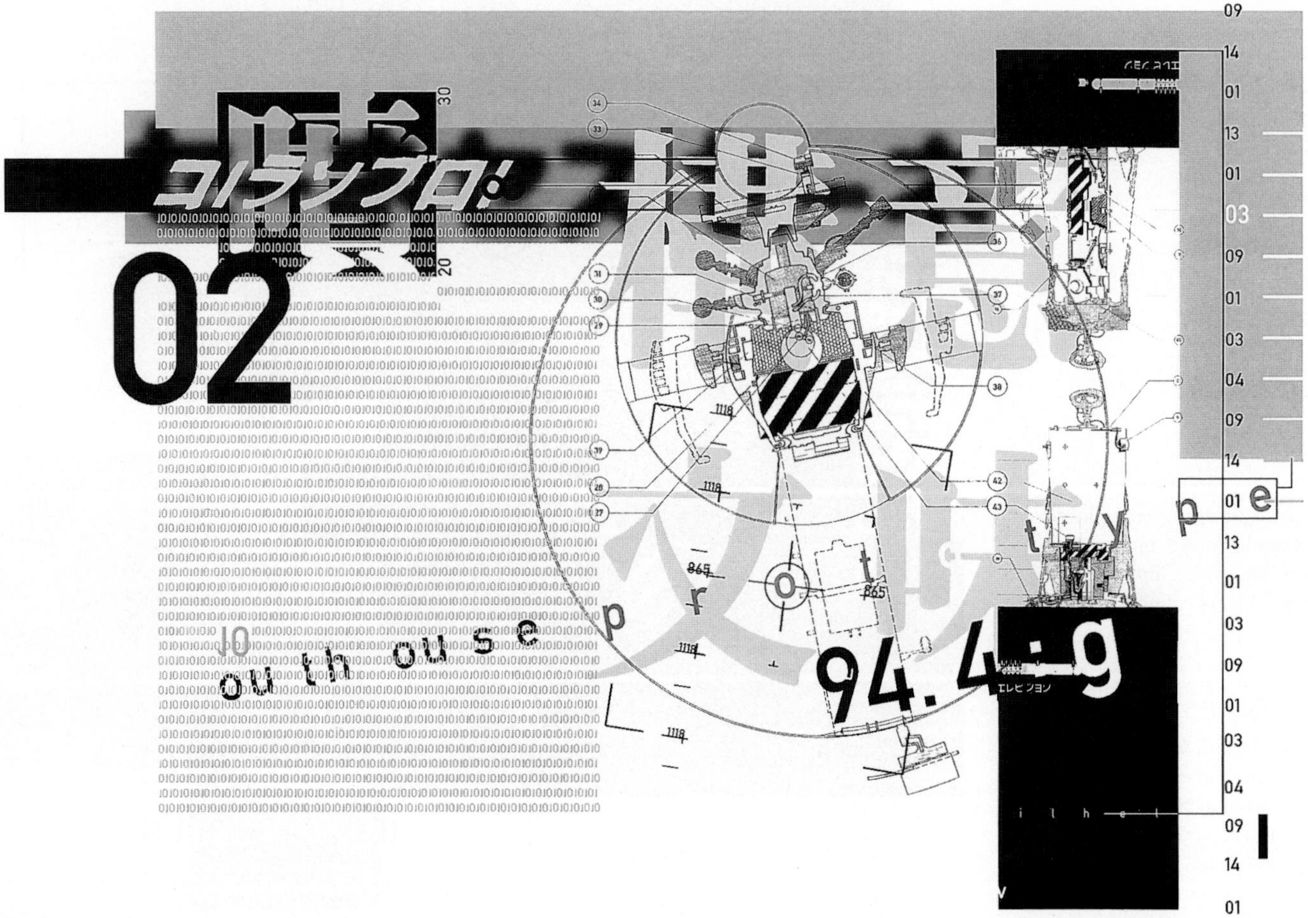

Drawing:
"Architextural" Composite. Visualization of kinetic, machine, indicator + targeting graphics, and deeply coded communication as an example of the synesis of the project. B+W electronic image integrating computer-manipulated, scanned, hand-drawn line work + images, orchestrated in QuarkXPress + Adobe Photoshop.

Design:
A kinetic public restroom facility in response to the lack thereof, within the New York and Los Angeles communities. Outhouse deconstructs itself after each paid usage. A completely self-sustainable project, the pissoir incorporates moveable interior/exterior video programming + display. The ARCHITECTURE exists only when in use, otherwise the object becomes urban street sculpture.

Drawing:

"Architextural" Composite. Visualization of kinetic, machine, indicator + targeting graphics, and deeply coded communication as an example of the RESONATING PENTAMETER of the project. Full-color electronic image integrating computer-manipulated, scanned, hand-drawn line work + images, orchestrated in QuarkXPress + Adobe Photoshop. 11" x 14" rainbow print.

Design:

Reader activated layout orchestrated to the musical structure of "2 Princes" (Spin Doctors). Text organized as datum indicated throughout the publication. The article involves cutting, folding, + overlapping of pages for visual consumption. Based on the idea of "Frozen Music," the historically 2D article becomes a 3D entity.

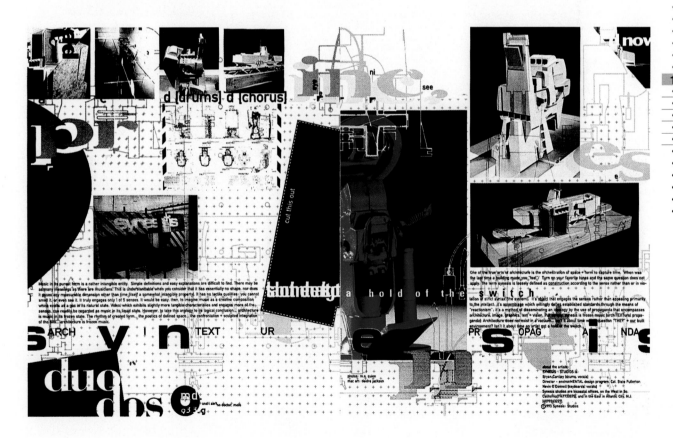

THE LAUGH : THE END

DRIVE-THRU SUPRE-MARkeT

The consumptive culture seeks to identify the means by which to make existence somehow easier. Assumably, it follows that our lives then must be difficult indeed. And so we search for ways to make the tasks of each day less cumbersome. If for the sake of argument, we identify *maintenance* as daily activities which one would undertake in order to live, i.e. shopping for groceries, picking up the drycleaning, making a withdrawal at the bank machine, having some film developed, filling the car up with gas, and perhaps even having the car washed. The proliferation of new building types have accomodated these desires. And yet, the strangeness of our innovations are somehow accepted without question, without scrutiny, without the laughter that might accompany the realization of the absurdity of our own devices.

The SUPRE-MArkeT is intended as an indexical account of the paralogical innovations which define our existence. Simply, the project is described as a continuous, spiraling bar of various programs grafted onto the freeway. In this ideal circumstance, the driver only slightly interrupts his commute home, actually steering the automobile directly into the interior space of the building. Once inside, a hydraulic mechanism, similar to what one might find in a car wash, pulls the car along, passing the Safeway, One Hour Cleaners, ATM machine, Foto-mat, Mobil, and the SUPRE-MArkeT Car Wash, finally re-emerging back onto the freeway, sparkling clean and filled to the brim with all the necessities that our daily lives require!

5 MPH

"Es muss sein, es muss sein, ja, ja, ja, ja!"
("it must be, it must be, yes, yes, yes, yes!")

VIEW OF SUPRE-MARKET

SECTION THRU ENTRY

INTERIOR PERSPECTIVE

The Story of the Drive-Thru SUPRE-MArkeT

In "The Unbearable Lightness of Being" Milan Kundera tells of an anecdote concerned with the notion of "it must be" or the famous Beethoven motif "Muss es sein? Es muss sein!" that speaks to the spirit and to the ultimate meaning of my proposal, THE LAUGH:

To paraphrase, it seems that a certain Dembscher owed Beethoven fifty florins. The composer, who was chronically short of funds, took to reminding him of the debt with a delightful little melody: "Es muss sein, es muss sein, ja, ja, ja, ja!" (or "It must be, it must be, yes, yes, yes, yes!) A year later, the same motif became the basis for the fourth movement of the last quartet, Opus 135. And so, Beethoven turned a frivolous inspiration into a serious piece of music, or "a joke into a metaphysical truth."

In other words, the concept of light to heavy, or a laugh turned inwards, may provide one with questions never ventured as prompting to answers heretofore ignored.

PARTIAL ELEVATION

SELECTED VIEWS   a   b   c   d   e   f   g

MODEL

AXONOMETRIC OF SITE

Drawing:

Composite. 30" x 30". Included in the array of drawings are: an interior perspective drawn in pencil, actual site photographs, a model photograph, an inked section and axonometric drawing and type-written text on clear adhesive. The base drawing was made by superimposing a model photograph onto the original image. The shadows were created using dot-screen adhesive tone.

Design:

Composite presentation seeks to give the viewer an understanding of unique existing condition created at the confluence of intersecting highways. The competition board layout re-creates these "snapshots" and arranges them in such a way that is reminiscent of the spiraling interior of the proposed building. The images reveal episodic events which depict specific aspects of the building which contrast with the Gestalt of the overhead superimposed view. In a way this experience is reiterated by the presence of the observation deck at the top of the Corning Tower which allows the usually car-bound spectator a similar sensation.

Drawing:

Composite assemblage. Mixed media on Sommerset Satin paper. Photograph, acrylic paint, bronzing powder, pastels. This assemblage represents one of a series of formulated mappings toward an investigation into the making of an Architecture. These constructs are "Transitional Objects" used to elucidate and represent an architectural thought which attempts to establish a poetic analogy and the potential for refiguration, resonance and meaning of the work of Architecture.

Design:

The project represented is a hybrid structure for one of Madrid's fastest growing peripheral settlements. The program includes a sacred space for 200 participants, meeting/classrooms, a parsonage and an exhibit/community hall. The building's two primary elements are a fragmented inclined concrete cylinder circumscribing an unearthed womb-like space, and a lighter steel and glass tower structure rising from within. The Sacred Space is suspended between the Community Hall on ground level and an interstitial space, defined by the superimposition of the two structural components.

plan fl 31

Ⓐ Ⓑ

WIND 30K /HR

VIEW TO OSAKA BAY

① LINE OF PROJECTION

②

LINE OF BUILDING FACE

KAWASAKI VOID – LOOKING THROUGH 31ST FLOOR

神戸

Cor-Tex / Neil M. Denari, California ▬
Neil M. Denari, assisted by Juan Garcia and Eric Chen
Kawasaki Void Competition, Kobe, Japan

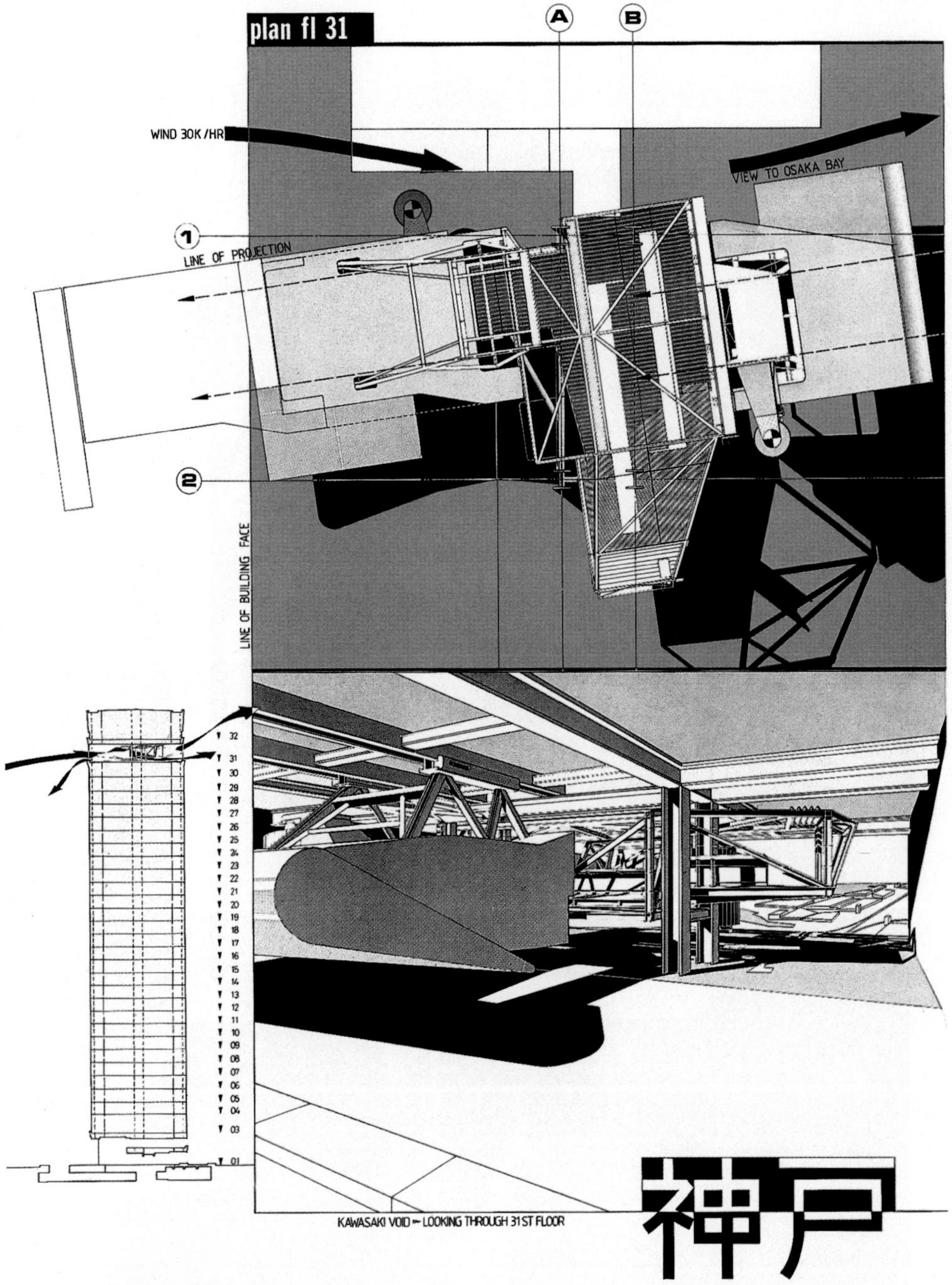

Drawing: ▬

Ink and adhesive dot screen on hand-drawn mylar original, with color film applied to a KC-5 print. The perspective was traced from a projected slide of a 1/8"-scale model. The shadows are extrapolated from a setting-sun position.

Design: ▬

The site is the 31st floor of the headquarters of the Kawasaki Heavy Industries Co. In using the constant 30K/hr. wind velocity at the 31st floor void space, two information projectiles operate on wind-generated power, each installed with a cylindrical turbine system. The nosecones move horizontally on tracks hanging from the structure above violating the vertical plane of the building. Once beyond the plane of the glass curtainwall, an INFO FIN unfolds to project and receive images, color, light, text, etc., to the city of Kobe. Between the animated elements is a glass space which is a small bar allowing the visitor to experience the disorienting effects of alcohol and technology.

Cor-Tex / Neil M. Denari, California
School 1992, Scheme 5

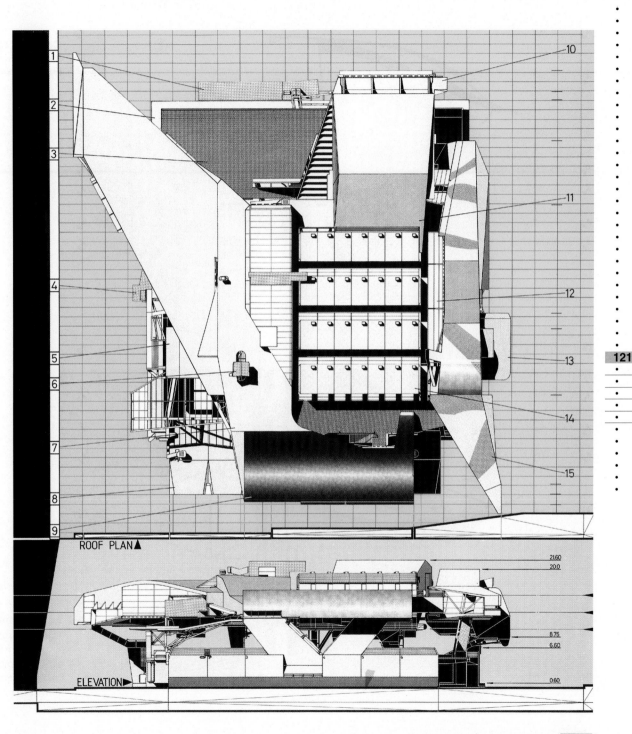

ROOF PLAN ▲

ELEVATION ▶

Drawing:

Adhesive dot screen on hand-drawn ink on mylar original, with pantone color film applied to a KC-5 print. The background grid in the roof plan section is both a neutral graphic and site field on which the building floats.

Design:

The HYPERactive integration of technology into the educational system has produced a NEW FORM OF LITERACY CHARGED BY THE IMMEDIATE ACCESS TO KNOWLEDGE and information storage systems. Often times physically interactive, technology is not far removed from the more traditional aspects of constructing artifacts in a convival atmosphere of learning. Architecture assumes, in the face of advanced technology, the role of spatializing the effects of events and situations which are temporal. In the school project, what has been considered most is the arrangement of the spaces of the collective human environment (work, play, discussion, etc.) as they collaborate with the spaces of technical serving (example: dense cores of individual computer laboratories violet open space; a grid of programmable ROBOTS assist the student in building physical models of heuristic value).

EL 59.20
EL 45.20
EL 27.60
EL 16.50
EL 12.60
EL 00.00
EL −05.80

EL 100.80
EL 85.20
EL 75.50
EL 67.40
EL 50.40
EL 33.40
EL 15.60
EL 00.00

Cor-Tex / Neil M. Denari, California ▬
Neil M. Denari, assisted by Laurence Turner and Kostas Manolides
Floating Illuminator

Drawing: ▬
Adhesive dot screen on hand-drawn ink on mylar original.

Design: ▬
Suspended from above, this object contains five light sources of varying degrees of intensity and quality. They are controlled by a hand-held remote unit which also operates as a rheostat and signaling device. A heat sensor activates the object within an 8-ft range. It is considered to be a floating fragment of a building. The object is constructed from break - formed 1mm steel sheet and 8mm aluminum rod with injection molded plastic reflector. Built by Cor-Tex.

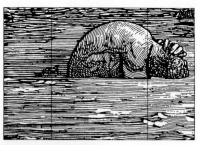
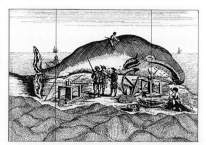
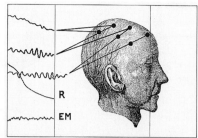

Dis/continuous Genealogy

Earth Mound •
Dante's *Inferno* XVII, reversed Doré' •
Monck's *Account of a Most Dangerous Voyage* •
Polygraphic recording of patient •
with independent narcolepsy •
Composite Ideogram •

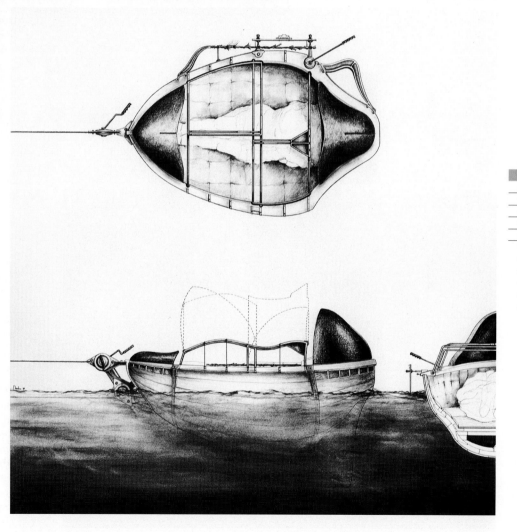

Douglas Darden, Associate Professor
University of Colorado, Denver, Colorado
Clinic for Sleep Disorders, A Rondo on the Study of Sleep

Drawings:

The Dis/continuous Genealogies represent a composite conceptualization of iconography, structure, formal composition, and program of the architectural project. The line drawings are ink on mylar film. The chiarscuro drawings (patient's boat) are graphite, graphite powder, gouache, and pastel on Stonehenge paper (from *Condemned Building,* Princeton Architectural Press).

Design:

Clinic for Sleep Disorders is slipped into the Morris Canal on the periphery of Liberty State Park, New Jersey. The canal empties into the Hudson River, west of lower Manhattan. Entry to the site is from a cobblestone road adjacent to an abandoned ferry terminal once used by commuters from New Jersey to Manhattan. The clinic plots for incoming patients a nearly cyclical course of travel through the canal and an existing hill.

123

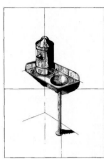
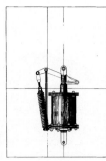
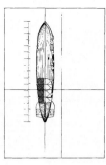

Dis/continuous Genealogy
- American Civil War Engraving
- Caboose Water Cooler and Basin
- Westinghouse Train Brake
- Hindenburg Zeppelin
- Composite Ideogram

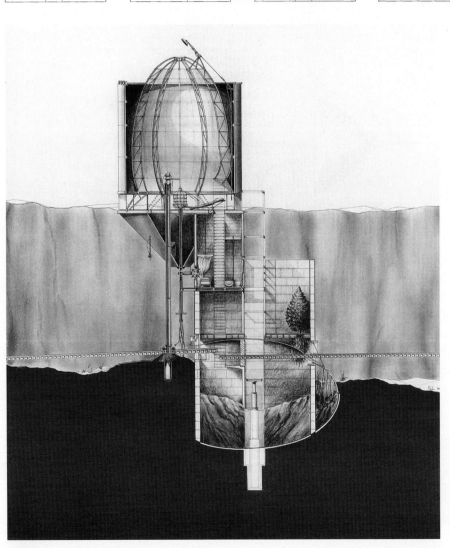

Douglas Darden, Associate Professor ■
University of Colorado, Denver, Colorado
Oxygen House, A Near Triptych on the Act of Breathing

Drawings: ■

The Dis/continuous Genealogies represent a composite conceptualization of iconography, structure, formal composition, and program of the architectural project. The line drawings are ink on mylar film. The chiarscuro drawing for the anatomical section is graphite, graphite powder, gouache, and pastel on Stonehenge paper (from *Condemned Building,* Princeton Architectural Press).

Design: ■

Oxygen House is perched on a depressed floodplain north-northwest of Frenchman's Bend, Mississippi. The structure is designed for Burnden Abraham, an ex-train signalman, who must live in an oxygen tent. In the early Spring of 1979, after torrential rains, the railroad tracks on which Abraham worked were flooded. They were never fully repaired. That following summer during a routine operation, Abraham suffered a collapsed lung when a train jumped the track and sent metal debris puncturing his right lung. Three years later the railroad company put the property up for sale. Abraham purchased the plot where he once had worked. He requested that his house be built over the scene of his near-fatal accident. Abraham also requested that he finally be entombed in the house.

Peter Edgeley, for Daryl Jackson Architects, Australia
Sega World, Darling Harbor, Sydney, Australia

Drawing:
Photomontage. Acrylic paint and airbrush on black card (20"x15").
The sky tones and the foreground water were airbrushed in first,
followed by the basic building forms painted over the top. Video
screens were then montaged in and further airbrush highlights
added last.

Design:
Sega World was looking at a proposal for a games and multi-media
center in Sydney. The design scheme and presentation for the
project convey the image of an electronic environment and activities related to video screens.

ARCHITECTURE **ELLERBE BECKET, New York in association with Quadrangle Architects, Toronto, Ontario, Canada**
Ellerbe Becket: Peter Pran, Design Principal; Timothy Johnson, Project Designer; Jeff Walden and David Koenen, Designers
Quadrangle Architects: Brian Curtner, Partner-in-Charge; Roland Rom Colthoff, Project Designer; Ted Shore and Wyn Bielaska, Designers; Micheal McCann, Watercolor Perspectivist
Tip Top Tailors - Waterfront Development, Toronto, Ontario, Canada

126

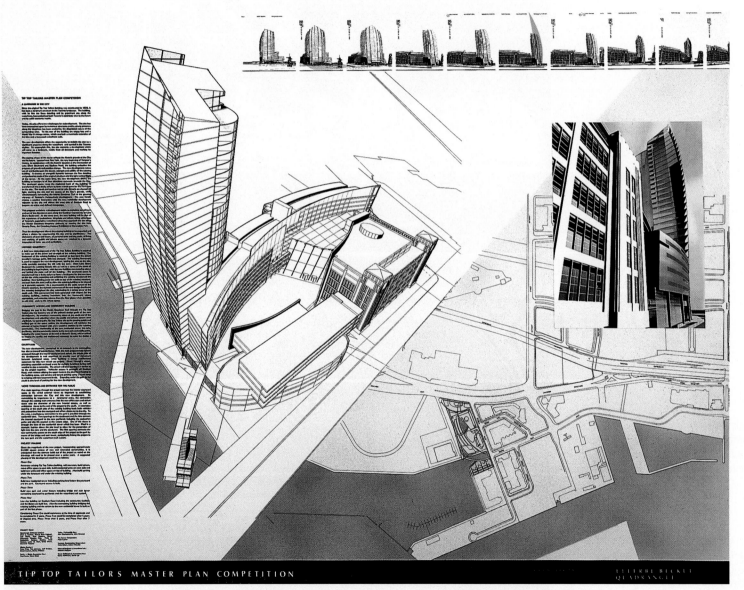

TIP TOP TAILORS MASTER PLAN COMPETITION

ELLERBE BECKET
QUADRANGLE

Drawing:

The drawings submitted as the winning entry to an International competition, were a composition of line drawings, three-dimensional computer-generated line perspectives, computer-generated renderings and watercolor perspectives. The intention was to combine techniques and mediums to best represent the multi-layered design collaboration and dynamic design intent.

Design:

The design integrates the existing warehouse located on the site with a new high-rise tower located adjacent to the waterfront with a sweeping curved mass of loft spaces. The result is the creation of a holistic yet fragmented central space which acts as an arrival court for the apartment tower and an interior atrium space for offices in the existing warehouse.

Design Team: Peter Pran, Design Principal; Curtis Wagner,
Ed Calma, Marla Wilthew and Timothy Johnson, Project Designers
State University of New York,
New Academic Buildings - Building A, Binghamton, New York

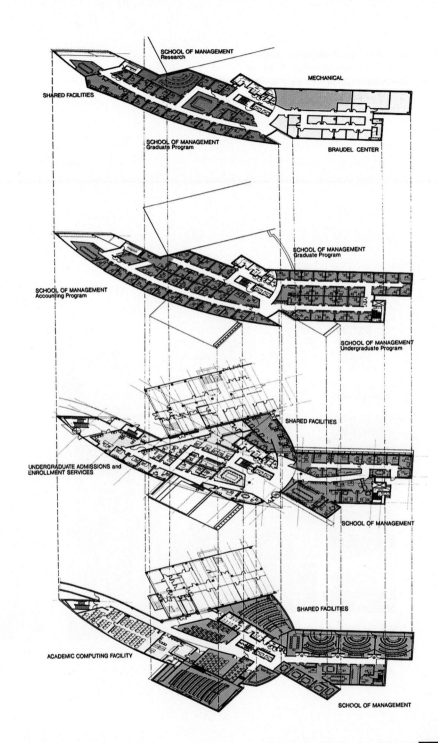

Third Floor

SCHOOL OF MANAGEMENT
Research

MECHANICAL

SHARED FACILITIES

SCHOOL OF MANAGEMENT
Graduate Program

BRAUDEL CENTER

Second Floor

SCHOOL OF MANAGEMENT
Graduate Program

SCHOOL OF MANAGEMENT
Accounting Program

SCHOOL OF MANAGEMENT
Undergraduate Program

First Floor

SHARED FACILITIES

UNDERGRADUATE ADMISSIONS and
ENROLLMENT SERVICES

SCHOOL OF MANAGEMENT

Ground Floor

SHARED FACILITIES

ACADEMIC COMPUTING FACILITY

SCHOOL OF MANAGEMENT

Drawings:

The exploded plan axonometric shows the complex sectional
relationships of various program spaces.

Design:

The existing State University of New York campus is dominated by
a series of rectilinear buildings on a 90° grid. The two new buildings
break the grid to create a dynamic expression of movement and
freedom. Building A, shown here in plan, leads one into the campus
with its curved facade.

Richard B. Ferrier, Professor
The University of Texas at Arlington, Texas
Observation Tower, Dallas Museum of Art "Architoy" Exhibit

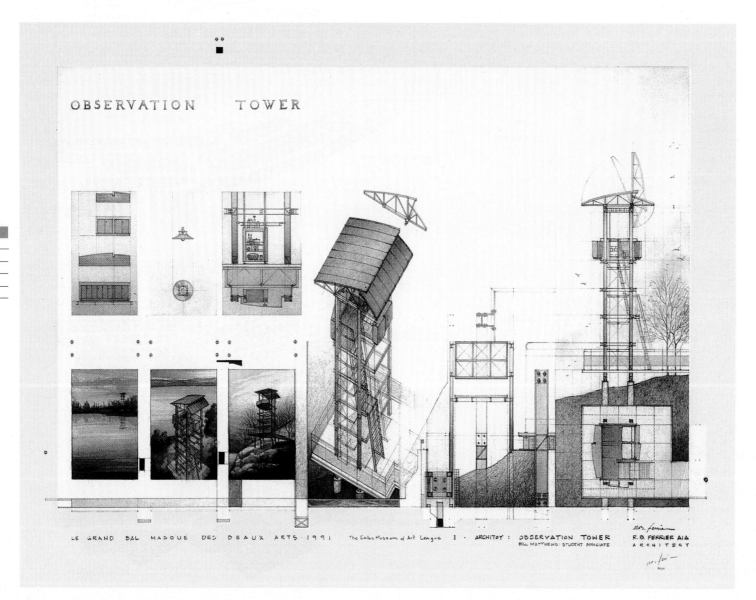

OBSERVATION TOWER

LE GRAND BAL MASQUE DES BEAUX ARTS 1991   The Dallas Museum of Art League   1 · ARCHITOY: OBSERVATION TOWER   R.B. FERRIER AIA
                                                                                    BILL MATTHEWS: STUDENT ASSOCIATE   ARCHITECT

Drawing:

Graphite, watercolor and metals on 300# D'Arches watercolor paper, 22" x 30". The central figure in this composition is an axonometric drawing of the tower and a typical roof truss. Plan, elevation and sectional detail drawings of various scales depict the character of the design. Three perspective views complete the diversity of image types and provide closure for the viewer wanting to know how the object might embrace the landscape. Metal bolts and nuts utilized for construction of the model are also employed as compositional elements in the drawing and literally attached through the surface of the watercolor paper.

Design:

The Dallas Museum of Art invited architects to participate in an "Architoy" exhibit. Drawings and models of architectural toys designed by the architects were exhibited and offered for auction.

Drawing: Serial space projection. Pen and ink black line drawing. Airbrush color and pasted colored paper. 594mm x 841mm.

Design: Vision is continually segmented, fragmented and obstructed by the overlapping walls of this design. Each person who traverses these various multilayered fragments is forced to patch them together through individual memory or perception to create a total link. The grid is inscribed with differences between parts that are multilayered and parts that are not multilayered. The grid is what people encounter when they search for the traces of differences.

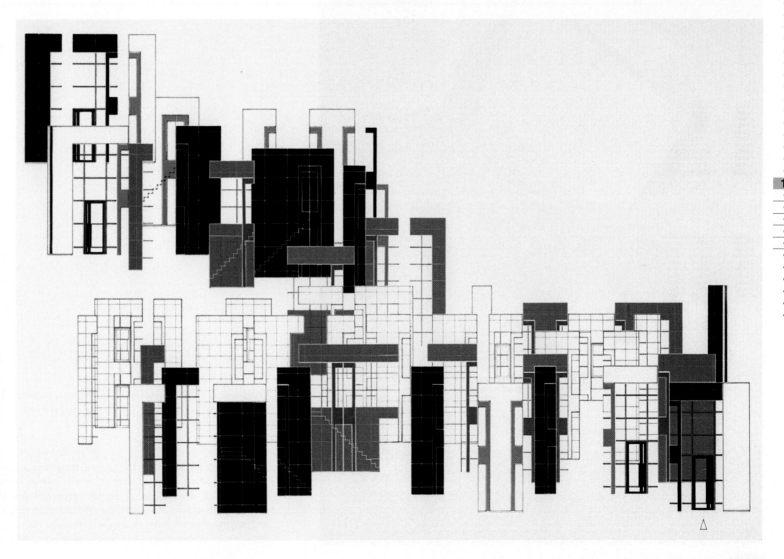

129

Gilbert Gorski, Renderer for Tate & Snyder Architects, Nevada ▬

Architect's Office, Henderson, Nevada

Drawing: ▬

Composite site plan and elevation. Referential site plan and elevation composed with implied layer of grids. Color pencil and airbrush on illustration board.

Design: ▬

The challenge for the design team was to maintain the spectacular views of the valley to the south while reducing solar heat gain on the glazing facing in this direction. The steep slope of the site suggested that the design could be multistory. In response to these issues the architects designed a building that is sculpted into the site to take advantage of the slope and views. It also incorporates passive solar design concepts to lessen the energy loads on the building.

Jawaid Haider, Ph.D., Associate Professor
The Pennsylvania State University, Pennsylvania
Evanston Public Library Competition

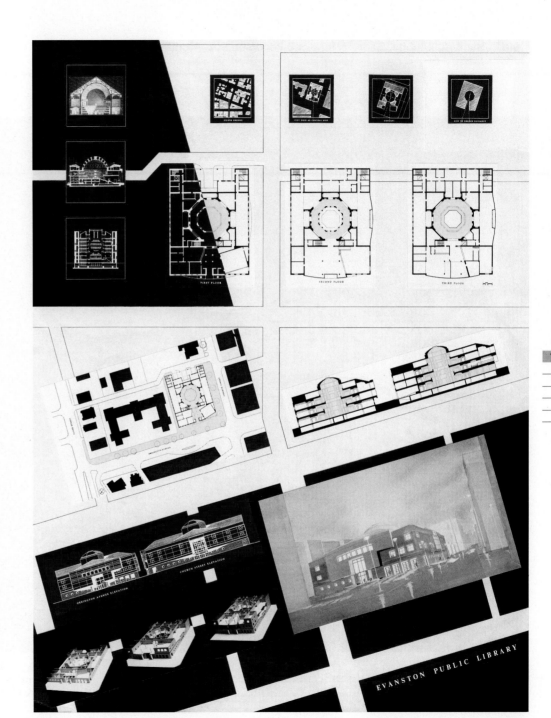

Drawing: The method used was similar to a collage technique. The site plan of the road network was drawn in ink on white paper. The black-and-white contrast was achieved by extending and accentuating the lines that define the shift in the city grid. All drawings were done in ink and reduced to fit the diagonal layout. Negatives of drawings on black background were produced photographically. The study model and the night-time perspective, which was rendered in watercolor, were photographed and reduced to appropriate size. Pantone was used to highlight significant spaces and spatial relationships in site plan, floor plans and sections.

Design: The site for the library presented an interesting shift in the city grid. This shift became an essential aspect of the design concept and the diagonal composition, which allowed the different drawings to read as one composite image.

131

InSite™

Drawing: ▬

The drawings were created in MacPerspective and a hidden line wireframe generated to match the perspective of site photograph. The wireframe was dropped into the scanned site image and rendered with textures cloned from the existing building. ColorStudio was used for all paint and rendering procedures were done on a Macintosh computer.

Drawing:
Composite board with perspectives, elevation, model photograph and a collage of aerial photographs and perspectival drawings. Use of people in the drawings give scale and suggests the program or event taking place in each space such as the "Bungee Jumping Ramp" for those impatient commuters who cannot wait any longer at the Transit Terminal Pier.

Design:
This project stems from a paradoxical human desire to be "connected" and "disconnected" from the city life at the same time. This proposal envisions the removal of the piers between Bay Bridge and Pier-39 including the existing ferry terminal, creating a "clear edge," opening a vista toward San Francisco Bay. The city is then re-created by a network of "dislocated" elements such as Transit Terminal Pier, Sunken Plaza, Stitch Bridges, and Fog Habitats.

PLAZA   OF   DISLOCATED   EVENTS

SAN FRANCISCO   EMBARCADERO   WATERFRONT

133

134

Drawing: ▬

Exploded perspective composite. Pen and ink on mylar, xeroxed onto ultra-white mylar and finished with colored Pantone films. 28" x 36". The technique of 'exploding' the perspective into layers allows the drawing to be simultaneously illustrative and conceptual. The illustrative aerial view is placed in a minimal context of mountain, river, rail, highway and sprawl. Reflecting the conceptual hierarchy, the 'armature' (utility rack/arcade and power plant) hovers above the open space network which in turn has primacy over massing and land use. (Homage is due to the offices of B. Tschumi and R. Meier.)

Design: ▬

The project is a transformation of a 19th century industrial 'site' into a 21st century corporate 'campus.' In addition to clarifying the existing site patterns, the primary cultural change is the creation of a network of active and passive recreational spaces. The entire campus is organized around a public space armature: a rectangular space composed of four major streets and utility racks which are reconfigured and augmented to include a pedestrian arcade.

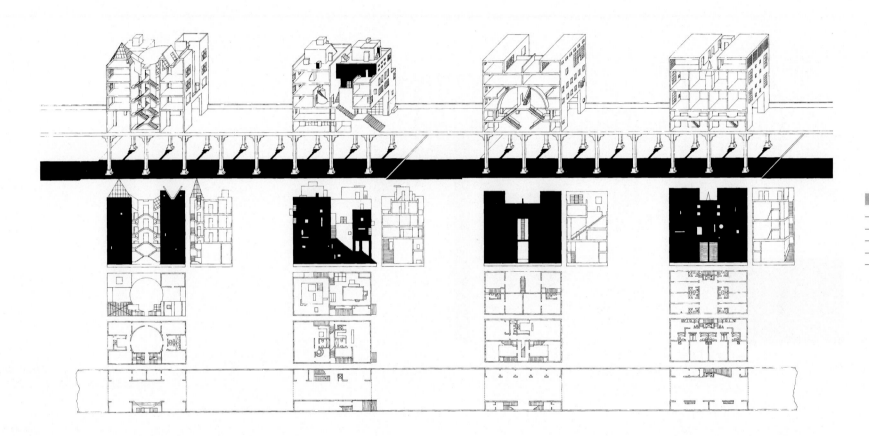

Drawing:
Composite plan, section and section-oblique. Pen and ink.

Design:
The site and structural foundation of the Bridge of Houses is the existing superstructure of an abandoned elevated rail link in the Chelsea area of New York. The structural capacity and width of the existing bridge determine the height and width of the houses. At one extreme are houses of single-room occupancy type, offered for the city's homeless. At the other extreme are houses of luxury apartments. Shops line the public promenade level below the houses.

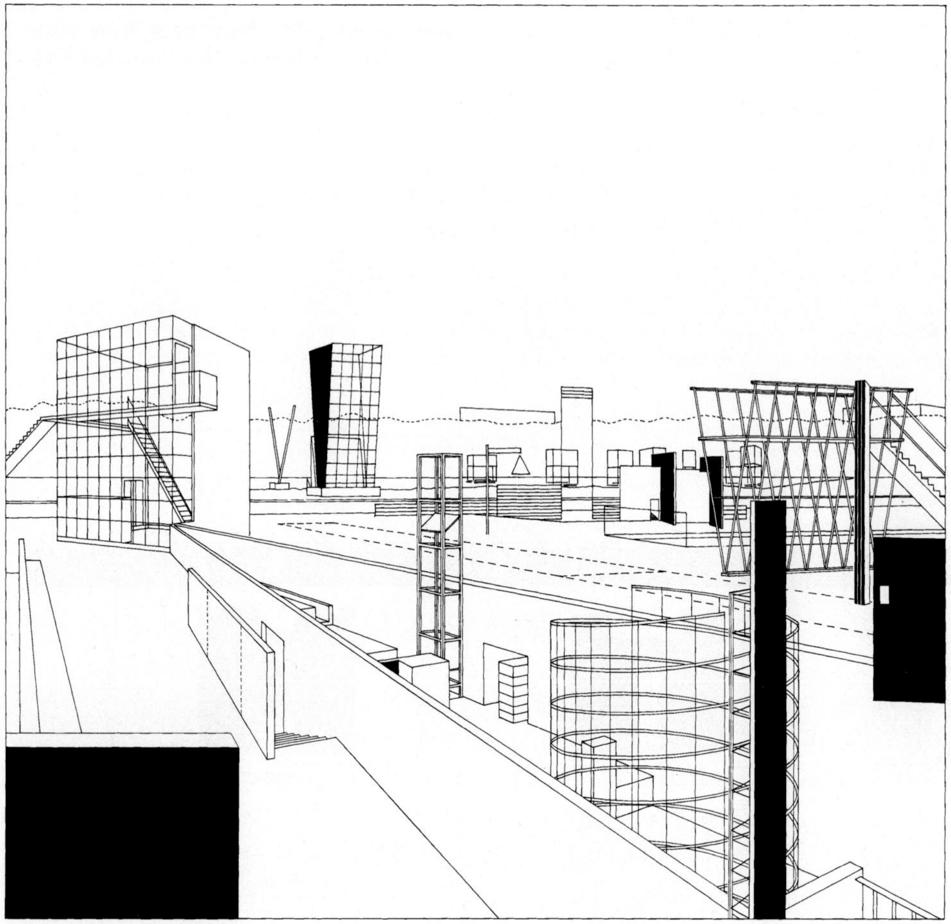

Steven Holl Architects, New York ━
Porta Vittoria, Milan, Italy

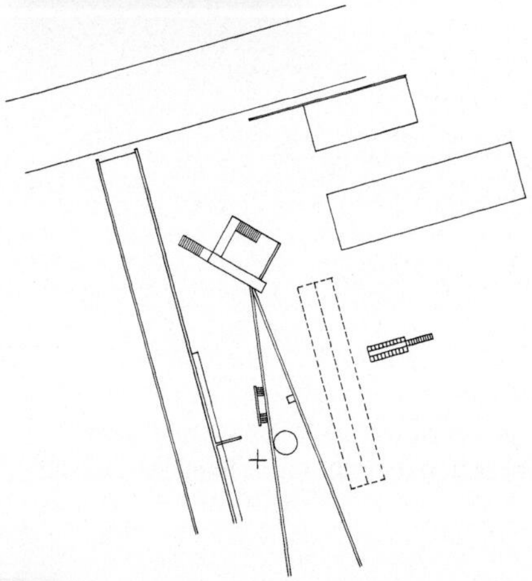

Drawing: ━
Plan and perspective. Pen and ink.

Design: ━
This proposal projects a new ring of density and intensity, adjoining the rolling green of a reconstituted landscape. The conviction behind this project is that an open work- an open future- is a source of human freedom. To investigate the uncertain, to bring out unexpected properties, to define psychological space, to allow the modern soul to emerge, to propose built configurations in the face of (and fully accepting) major social and programmatic uncertainty: this is the intention for the continuation of a "theoretical Milan."

136

Drawing:

Axonometric and plan composite. Pencil, prisma-color and spray paint on 32"x32" vellum. The rendering is about texture, color and the various aspects of design, both in plan and elevation. The axonometric view is rendered in pencil on the front side of vellum to suggest the texture of materials. Colored pencil is used on the back so that the subtle richness of color shows through without the brightness of heavily rendered color. The same technique is used on the background plane which helps to emphasize the smaller elements and gives the drawing as a whole a ground to stand on.

Design:

In the serenity of a secluded site in the Sierra foothills, this contemporary farmhouse has its historic roots in a fictional compound of rural buildings connected over the years into a rambling house. The natural colors of the surrounding vegetation take focus as the burgundy front door and wood floor match shades of manzanita bark while the blue-green wash of the kitchen cabinets derives from the lichen on oak trunks just outside. Boldly trimmed windows capture natural composition and complex shapes and surprising materials invite the imagination to soar.

137

House+House Architects, California ━━
David Haun, Renderer
Ka Hale Kakuna, Maui, Hawaii

Drawing: ━━

Axonometric, plan and elevation composite. India ink and airbrush on 26"x48" mylar. The rendering is a composite of drawings graphically laid out around the geometries of the plan and interrelated through a system of regulating lines. By using multiple images it is possible to understand the building plan and spatial characteristics within the framework of a single drawing. The precision of pen and ink was needed to allow for the finer features to read clearly.

Design: ━━

A massive curving wall anchored in lava cliffs encircles and protects a tropical retreat on the island of Maui. By turning its back on the intense south and west sun, the house caters to clients who desired a site-specific home that expresses the tropical island's unique character and lifestyle. Indoor and outdoor spaces are inseparably linked with disappearing walls which open each room onto outdoor lanais. Intricate screens cast glittering patterns of light and shadow as they trace the sun's path, while tropical vegetation cascades down the lava cliffs and spills inside. A tower links the two wings and offers distant views to the volcano of Haleakala and the Pacific Ocean beyond.

Franklin D. Israel Design Associates, California
Tisch-Avent • Culver City, California

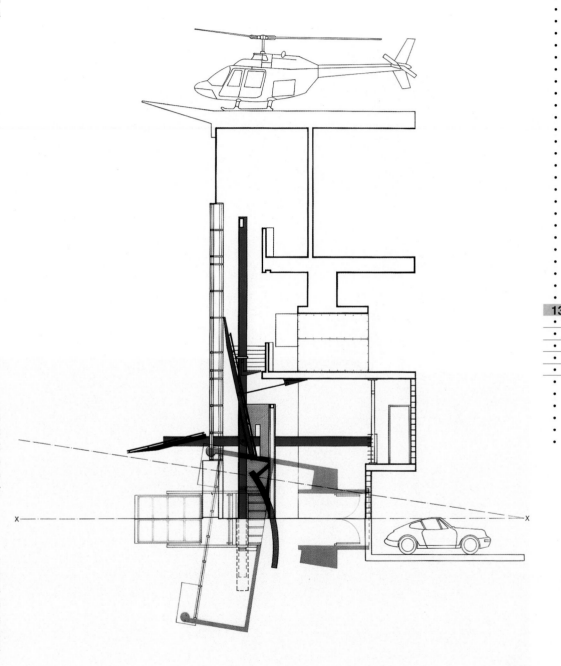

Drawing:

Entry wall + canopy plan-section-elevation. This drawing conveys an intervention in the triple height section of the entry space; the implied activities of the inner spaces beyond as well as the scale of the building (helicopter on the roof). The existing condition of the base building is drawn in ink on mylar with the intrusion of the entry and canopy piece rendered in color. Pantone films applied onto pin-bar mylar to register with the ink drawing. *Drawing by Lindy Roy.*

Design:

A steel-and-glass canopy extends to the exterior from the three-story lobby, creating a new entrance for the building. While filling the lobby, the canopy extends from the ground level up into the producer's office level and the associate's level above it. Set at an angle that follows the line of movement from the street into the main level of the building, the axis is terminated vertically by an occulus that aligns with a tunnel leading to a three-story conference room. The occulus also fills the third floor reception space with natural light.

140

Drawing:

Entry wall + canopy plan-section-elevation. This drawing describes an entry composed of a large curved wall, an asymmetrically supported canopy and the intersecting arrival stairs. The technique conveys the tectonics and mathematical nature of construction of these elements. Pin-bar registration is used to combine the positive and negative ink on mylar image into one drawing. *Drawing by Tom Rael.*

Design:

A low "V" marks the entrance to the headquarters, and a long curving outer wall presses out toward the street. The billowing curve coyly suggests that Virgin may be more "pregnant" with inspiration than its name would indicate. Though no longer affronted by the multivalent architectural machismo of the site on Main Street in Venice, the Virgin complex in Beverly Hills fends off the cool advances of her neighbors with graceful composure.

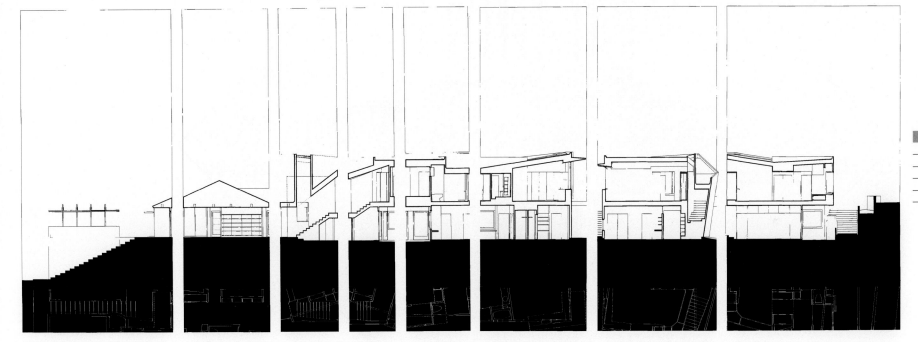

Drawing:
Sequential plans + sections. This drawing documents the sequence of space moved through from the arrival at the existing house downhill; progressing in a spiral fashion within the addition, coming upon a large corner window directed toward the only view of Silverlake; and culminating at the sleeping porch window looking uphill. The drawing is achieved by splicing ink on mylar originals with fragments of plan negatives. *Drawing by Annie Chu and Rick Gooding.*

Design:
A 1400-foot addition to a bungalow on the north side of Silverlake, the Woo Pavilion adds a few new dimensions to the notion of a "Pavilion in a Garden." The design tried to reflect the gentle and enlightened philosophy of the clients in the exterior disposition of the pavilion and its placement on the site. The pavilion was pulled to one side of the property, improving its view of Silverlake and allowing an open, outdoor "room" on the other side. Clad in stone-washed stucco, the walls of the addition appear to buckle and pull away in places, revealing and illuminating an interior world.

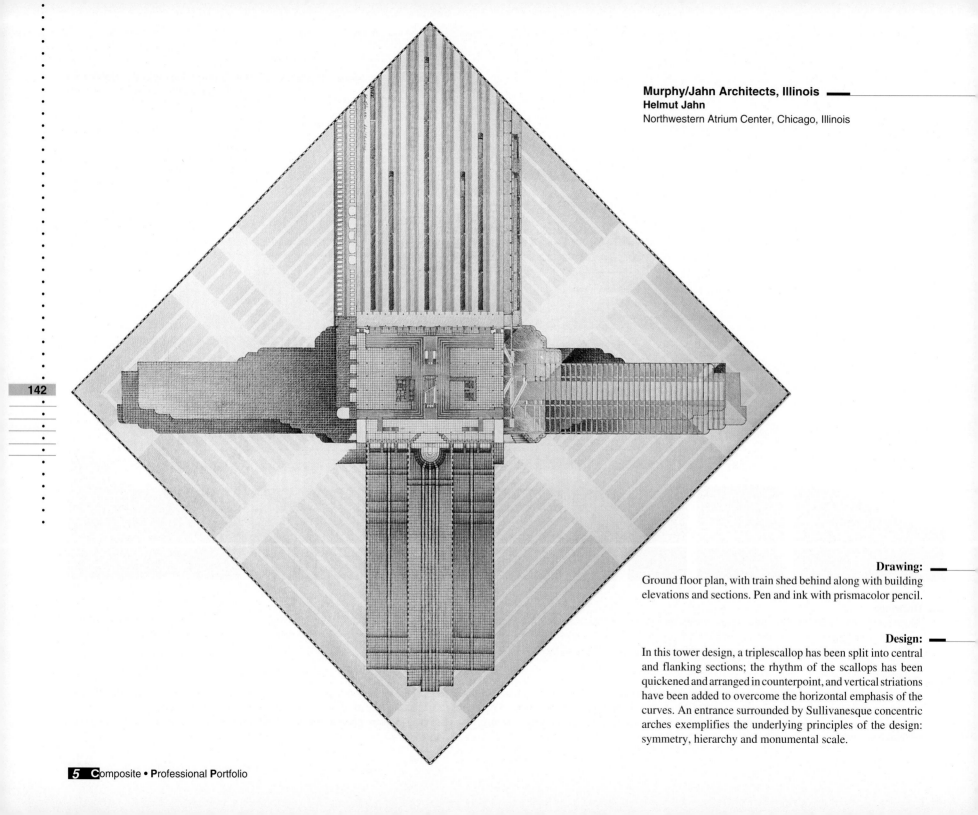

Murphy/Jahn Architects, Illinois ▬
Helmut Jahn
Northwestern Atrium Center, Chicago, Illinois

Drawing: ▬
Ground floor plan, with train shed behind along with building
elevations and sections. Pen and ink with prismacolor pencil.

Design: ▬
In this tower design, a triplescallop has been split into central
and flanking sections; the rhythm of the scallops has been
quickened and arranged in counterpoint, and vertical striations
have been added to overcome the horizontal emphasis of the
curves. An entrance surrounded by Sullivanesque concentric
arches exemplifies the underlying principles of the design:
symmetry, hierarchy and monumental scale.

Murphy/Jahn Architects, Illinois
Helmut Jahn
O'Hare Rapid Transit Station
O'Hare International Airport, Chicago, Illinois

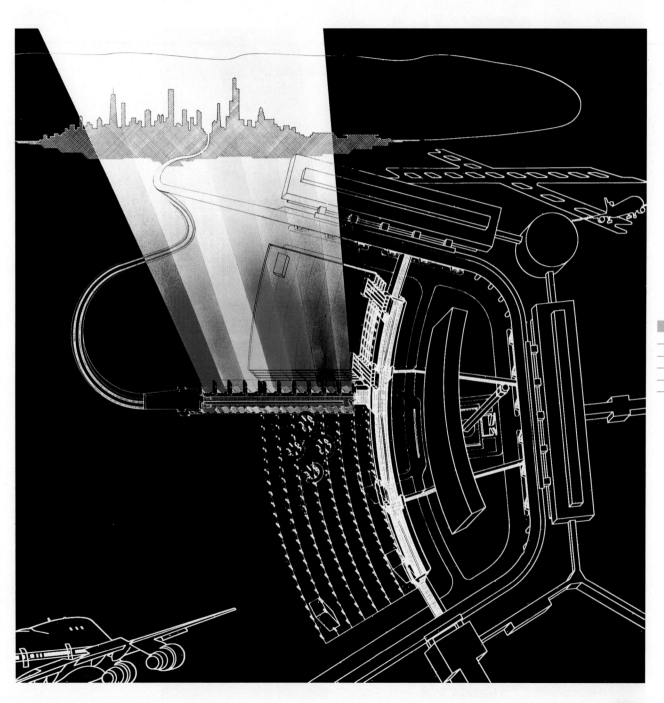

Drawing:
Urban transit station at Chicago O'Hare Airport showing connection from airport to city, the gateway to Chicago. Pen and ink drawing printed reverse on KP-5 paper. Airbrush color added on KP-5 print.

Design:
Located on the airport grounds under the main parking structure, the construction involved not only an open cut excavation lined with sloping sprayed concrete berms but also post-tensioned concrete girders to transfer the load from the columns above. The berms became the starting point of a design that is deliberately and enthusiastically decorative (berms painted in a rainbow of colors, transparent and translucent undulating glass block walls, etc.).

144

Murphy/Jahn Architects, Illinois ▬
Helmut Jahn
"Projects 1992"

Drawing: ▬

Collage. Four color lithograph. Original sketches in pen and colored ink with prismacolor.

Design: ▬

Design study sketches of various projects worked on during the year 1992.

Drawing:

Computer graphics composite image. 3D solid model was produced on CATIA during the design process. Rendering was completed on inhouse "REALS" ray tracing software. Photomontage by Shimatronix graphics paint system. Output format includes digitally produced print, slide and 4x5 positive. Presentation panel for competition. 2048 x1360 pixels.

Design:

Established at a ruin site within the city, the memorial becomes an amphitheater where the entire town is the stage, visible through clear screens containing liquid crystal cores. Visitors can relax on the tiered circular seating with their backs to the center and observe the actual town or images of the past overlaid on the present. "Media towers" laid out in a grid pattern on the site and extending into the town have multiple functions of recording and playback of sound and images, image projection, hologram projection, weather data recording, etc.

Kajima Corporation, Tokyo, Japan ▬▬▬
Design: A. Scott Howe & Tomohito Okudaira • Renderer: A. Scott Howe
Office Building, Tokyo, Japan

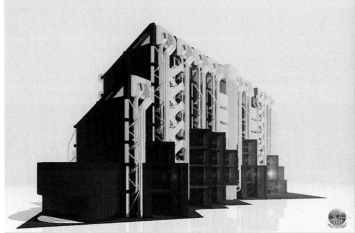

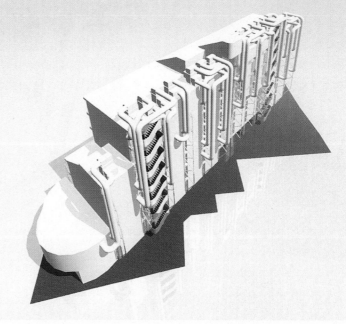

146

Drawing: ▬▬
Computer graphics multi-view perspective. 3D solid model was produced on CATIA during the design process. Rendering was completed on inhouse "REALS" ray tracing software. Output format includes digitally produced print, slide and 4x5 positive. Each image 1024 x688 pixels.

Design: ▬▬
Floors two through four function as a library, with offices on floors five through seven. The front of the building responds to the street with conventional curtain wall construction while the entire rear facade becomes a truss wall containing core elements: elevators, exterior stairways, restroom modules, and exposed mechanical equipment. Angular study nooks protrude through the truss wall on the library floors.

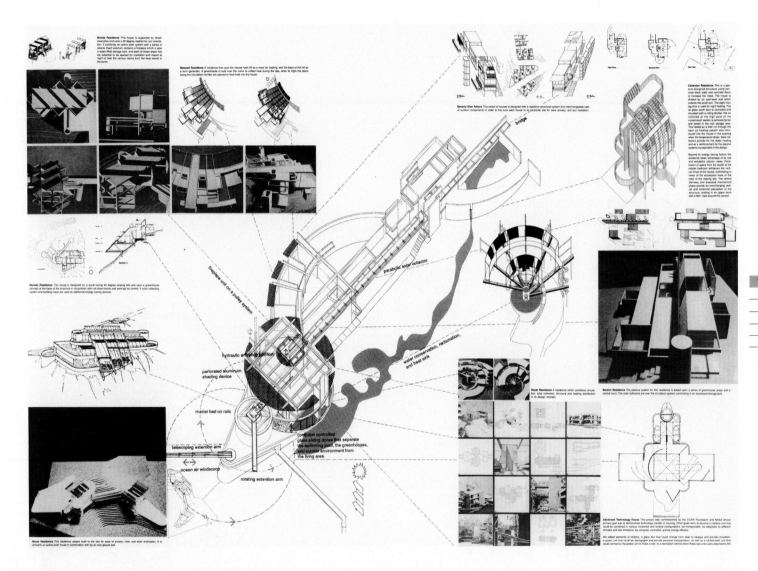

147

Drawing: Hybrid integrated presentation representing design process. Structural axonometric overlaid with the energy control and kinetic aspects of design. Photographs of models and drawings added with lines connected to the original drawing representing connections to previous work and ideas.

Design: A residential design that attempts to incorporate many ideas that the architect has worked on for the past forty years with emphasis on systems, kinetics, energy, and self-sustaining methods. Emphasis is upon continuum in the work rather than one-off design concepts.

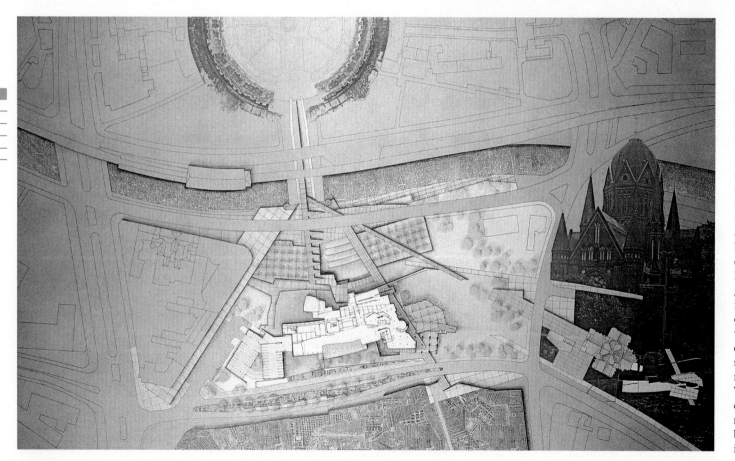

Drawing:
The site plan shows the relationship and the forces that the existing library and new addition have with the surrounding area. The drawing is a collage of newsprint, airbrushed color and pen and ink on Strathmore paper. *Drawn by William Calahan.*

Design:
(This image and the one on page 149): The facilities of the new building are a composition of functional elements arranged to generate visual and physical access to the existing building and surrounding points of interest of the Blucherplatz. The integration of the new building is achieved by placement of the sculpted forms of the new auditorium and punctured planes of the cafeteria walls across the front of the complex. The circulation zone is a transparent shaft which serves the floor plates and projects toward a neighborhood church with a glass-enclosed ramp connecting each level. The concrete structural grid of the new library is shifted in response to the axial forces of the site. The glass curtain wall is articulated by the use of different colors of glass responding to the library stack modules of the typical floor. The aluminum-framed wings of perforated metal deflect the north view and screen the library space from public activity in the plaza below.

Drawing:
The drawing is a collage of site plan and front elevation, illustrating the forces that come to bear on the building. The site plan was printed on Strathmore paper and the elevation drawn with ink and colored with airbrush and colored pencil. The softness of coloring allows a clear reading of the concrete, aluminum and glass of the building. *Drawn by William Calahan.*

Design:
Refer to site plan drawing.

150

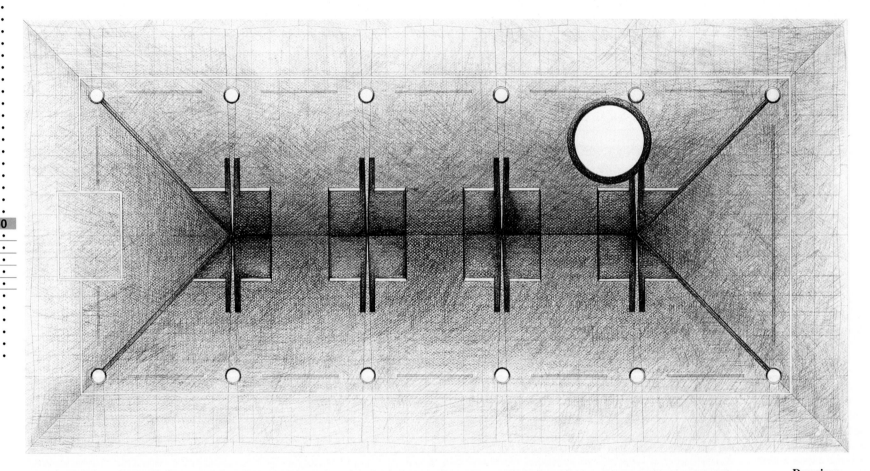

Drawing: ▬

Hung-ceiling plan. Pencil on Watson paper. 1520mm x 2360mm. Drawing showing ceiling tiles and curved metallic plating that resemble an airplane wing.

Design: ▬

On top of this underground photography museum the roof was designed to look as if it were suspended from the heavens. The first floor would contain only the entrance hall and tea room, and all four walls would be made of glass to emphasize the feeling of lightness and transparency. Seen from the outside, the intended effect with the transparent glass was for the room to look as if it were floating, since only the roof would be visible.

David Leary & Laura Owen, Kentucky
Choragic Monument to Twentieth Century Architecture

Drawing:
Independently executed color photographs and freehand graphite drawings were reassembled to construct a static image of a dynamic "monument."

Design:
Damaged technological objects and evocative projected images are juxtaposed to create a theoretical analogy which characterizes this century's "vast array of creative flux."

George S. Loli, Associate Professor of Architecture
University of Southwestern Louisiana, Lafayette, Louisiana
Villa ad Aggate (Varese), Italy

152

Drawing:
Oil pastel over pencil sketch.

Design:
Preliminary design concept for a large villa with the intention of the roof being a terrace and swimming pool combined.

Lubowicki/Lanier Architects, California
Susan Lanier & Paul Lubowicki
O'Neill Guesthouse, Brentwood, California

Plan and Elevations

Drawing:

These drawings are based on the Krazy Kat comics by George Herriman and are meant to evoke the Sunday Comics. The process started with original ink and zip-a-tone color drawing which was scanned and printed by Nash Editions on computer. The background drawings are silkscreen cartoon images on a hand-made paper over which was silkscreened a swath of clear coat creating a frame onto which the computer image was printed. Additional drawings were possible to scan and rearrange onto the paper making this an additive process which can continue to evolve.

Design:

The architectural language is based on the associative meaning derived through juxtapositioning symbolic elements. Similar elements were designed to express dissimilar qualities. Dissimilar elements were designed to express "related" qualities. They co-exist to intensify the various aspects of interiority and exteriority (i.e., Can one experience being within the garden and within an architectural enclosure at the same time?). One's experience of the site extends this dialogue further by addressing two worlds simultaneously: the neighborhood/street and the garden. Both worlds are comprised of like elements. The world belonging to the neighborhood/street consists of a front yard, the existing house, a rear garden deck bordered by a pool. It is joined by a bridge over the pool to the world of the garden: the guesthouse, a lower garden, and a creek.

THE TOWER STRIPPED BARE BY TIME EVEN

Lupo / Rowen Architects, New York ▬▬
Frank Lupo, Daniel Rowen
Times Square Tower, New York

Drawing: ▬▬ ▬▬

Photocomposite drawing. Reversed ink on mylar drawing combined with enlarged negative postcard image of Times Square. Clear film overlays of text and reduced ink drawing of axonometric view, wing mechanism. Airbrushed search lights.

Design: ▬▬

First prize winner of Times Tower Competition. Giant movable video wings that opened at dusk and closed at dawn over Times Square broadcasting news and special interest programming from around the world to the crowds below.

Machado and Silvetti Associates, Inc., Massachusetts
David Cowan, Christopher Doyle, Renderers
Tower of Leonforte: Four Public Squares, Leonforte, Sicily

Drawing:
The construction of the Tower of Leonforte at Four Public Squares. Composite drawing of city plan of Leonforte, tower sections, elevations and perspective views from the tower and of the tower. Ink on Strathmore paper.

Design:
The Tower of Leonforte is the focal point of an urban design proposal to unify the city. Outlined on the tower is the Gran Fonte, the historic 17th century fountain of Leonforte. Telescopes and viewing devices aimed at important buildings and public spaces pierce the structure.

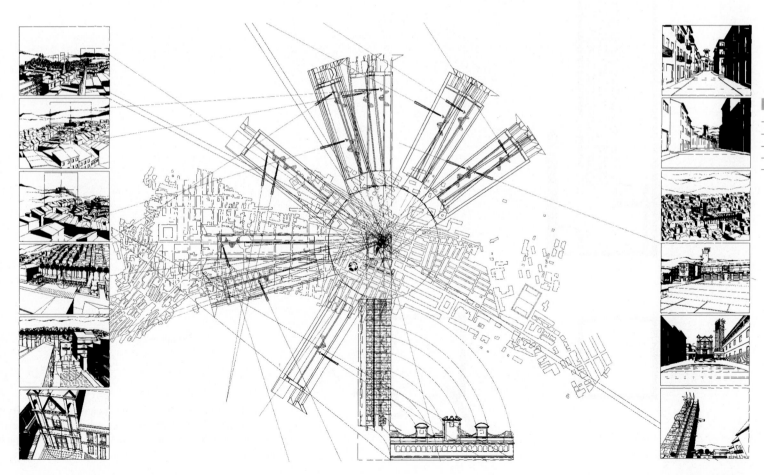

155

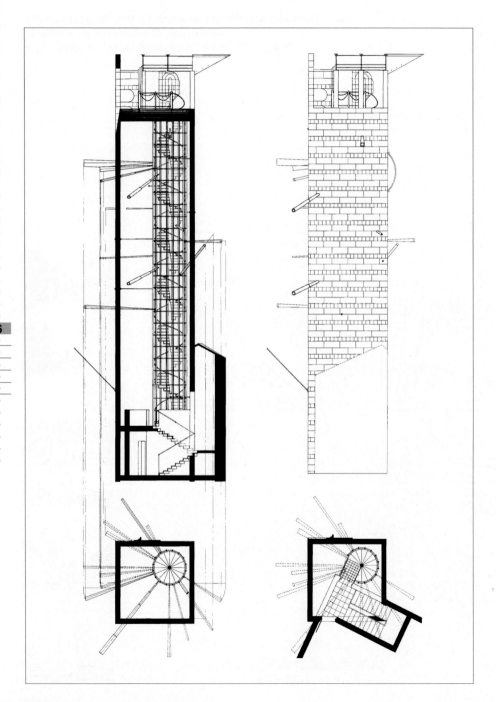

Machado and Silvetti Associates, Inc., Massachusetts ▬
David Cowan, Christopher Doyle, Renderers
Tower of Leonforte: Four Public Squares, Leonforte, Sicily

Drawing: ▬
Composite plan, section and elevation. Ink on Strathmore paper.

Design: ▬
The Tower of Leonforte is a new monument for the city. It contains a spiral stair and numerous telescopes and viewing devices that pierce the wall and focus on specific events in the city. At the top of the tower is a fountain which occasionally overflows.

Mack Architects, California
Mark Mack
Adelman/Llanos House, Santa Monica, California

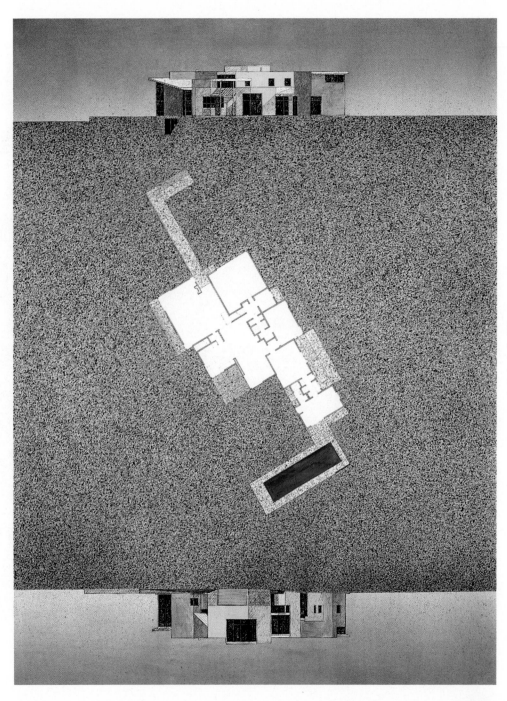

Drawing:
Composite plan and elevations. Pen and ink, airbrush color on white board.

Design:
Three main concepts animate the Adelman/Llanos design. The house is composed of interlocking and notched spaces, including expansive corner windows whose configuration and placement represent an attempt to control sun and sight lines toward trees and sky rather than the nearby houses. The house also forms an "L" footprint along two perimeters in order to gain maximum southern exposure and to leave a large backyard for the pool and patio. Finally the design sought to banish the typical suburban typology of a house fronted by a garage by making a large master suite over the garage, separated from the living-room area both by color and by the entry that divides the two volumes.

David Thomas Mayernik, New York
Villa Dedicated to the Four Seasons

Drawing:

An analytique drawing that combines both a layered and an assembled compositional strategy. It creates an illusion of the real while acknowledging itself as an image on paper. Pencil and watercolor on Arches cold press. Watercolor paper 18"x21".

Design:

Classical humanist culture has always been deeply rooted in the products and cycles of the natural world. This project posits an ideal villa just outside the urban realm, and between the field and the garden. It is both a contemplative retreat and an active center of agricultural production.

159

Drawing:
Montage 32"x36".

Design:
This competition entry for the Performing Arts Theaters at the Los Angeles Arts Park was primarily focused on the issue of how to juxtapose man-made objects with nature. In the design solution, articulated pieces of the structure are visible to passersby, configured in such a way as to invite further exploration. The majesty and power of the arts is about what goes on at a deeper level than what is outwardly apparent. The building, more than half buried, is revelatory in the sense that where there is a visible part of the building, it is sculptural and kinetic in nature. Buildings set within 200-acre, park-like setting now become functional sculptures in keeping with the overall Artspark concept.

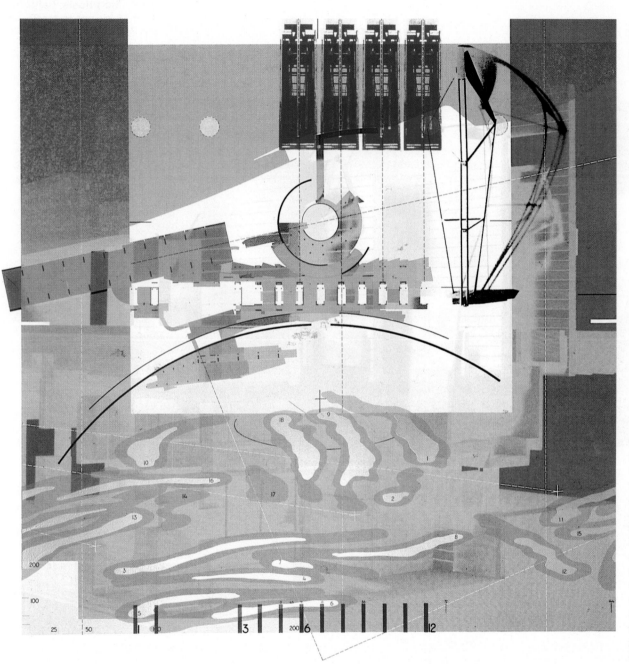

Morphosis, California
Thom Mayne, with
Christopher Wahl and John Nichols, Printmakers
Golf Club at Chiba Prefecture

Drawing:
Serigraph on Arches 88. 24"x24".

Design:
The entire program with it's emphasis on the *game* (golf) is about movement, the rhythm of walking, the arc of an arm in full swing, the nature and sequence of physical spaces, the narrative and diversity of place, and the dynamic and connective nature of organization. The building is about the land's surface (here it's orientation to the building's sectional characteristics) as it affects movement both through the automobile and through the pedestrian. The basic Parti is made up of four elements: a segment of a curved wall which produces a space for arrival (automobile), a lineal sequence of alternating volumes which accommodates a majority of the program, a second circular wall which embraces the larger site and facilities movement to the grounds, and a pavilion which contains space for dining and social events.

Morphosis, California
Thom Mayne with Sarah Allan
Blades Residence

Drawing:
Schematic section and plan. Graphite on 12"x12" mylar.

Design:
The building arrangement, while alluding to the specific characteristics of this site, ultimately demonstrates its tentativeness to fixity by making overt reference to our temporary status as occupants.

161

Eric Owen Moss Architects, California
Eric Stultz, Computer Renderer
Stealth Theater and Offices

162

Drawing: ▬
Computer composite. Building on site.

Design: ▬

The project is defined first by the location of the excavation for the petrochemical waste removal. The garden/court is located in the excavated area, minimizing refill of the hole. Inside the old bow-string structure, the "black box" theater faces the sunken garden seating, with the option of seating on both sides of the stage forming a "theater in the round." The design of the office building reuses Heraclitus: You never step into the same form twice. The north end of the building is three sided. The south end is four sided. The ends are simple, geometric, recognizable. Between the ends, the building section varies constantly over its length. The ends are known; in-between is not. The aspiration is to make a building which is constant and constantly moving, evolving like the cleaned-up site and the reused industrial buildings.

Eric Owen Moss Architects, California
Paul H. Groh, Computer Renderer
Ibiza Paseo, Ibiza, Baleares, Spain

163

Drawing:
Computer composite. Building on site.

Design:
The conceptual method of the project is to posit a design beginning without knowing the end. The building was designed one step at a time, with each step (contains aspects of space, form, structure, material, site, circumstance, and program) as an amendment to the previous step and a forecast of what might follow. The project aspires to suggest a sensibility, conscious of tradition, that simultaneously enjoys its stretching and remodeling.

164

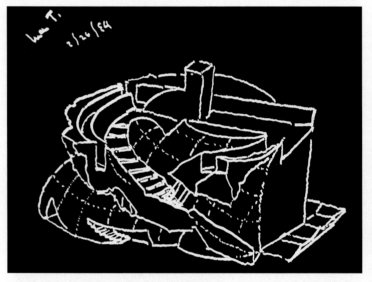

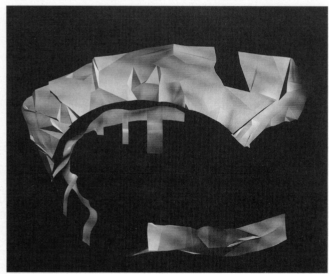

Drawing: ▬

Freehand sketch and computer drawings. *Sketch by Eric Owen Moss.*

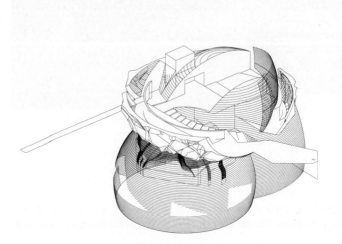

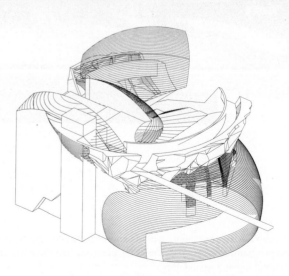

Design: ▬

The new 450-seat cinema and live performance "theater-in-the-park" is both a sociological and an aesthetic hypodermic to the prosaic replanning of the derelict east end of Culver City. The theater form originates with the conjunction of three spheres. Irregular surfaces insulate the exterior cinemas acoustically, deforming the roof sphere. Another series of acoustic panels amend the internal geometry of two spheres below.

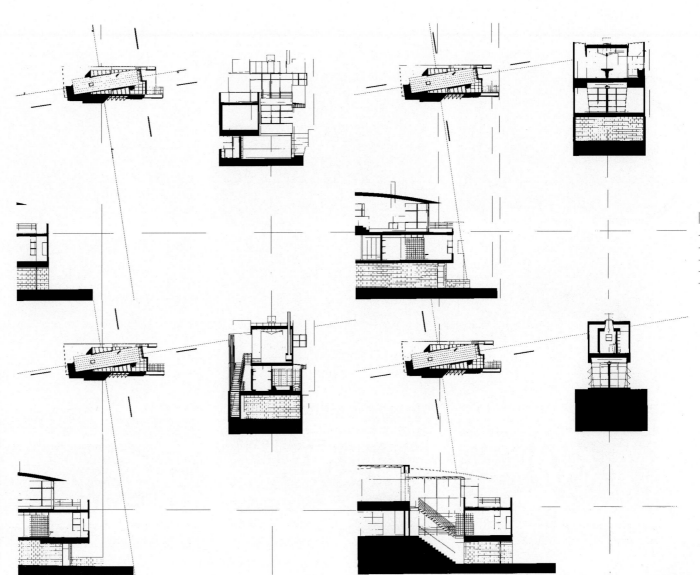

165

Drawing:
Composite sequential sections. Ink on mylar.

Design:
This small house located in a neighborhood on the edge of transformation, in a beachfront community on the edge of Los Angeles. Adjacent structures, which taken individually are quite unremarkable, together form an urban edge and demand an architectural response. The building is conceived of as an abstraction of borrowed neighborhood elements, and an experience of the light, view and climate that is fundamental to life at the beach in Los Angeles.

Pollari x Somol, Chicago, Illinois
Centrum Nova, Glosses. Competition Entry.

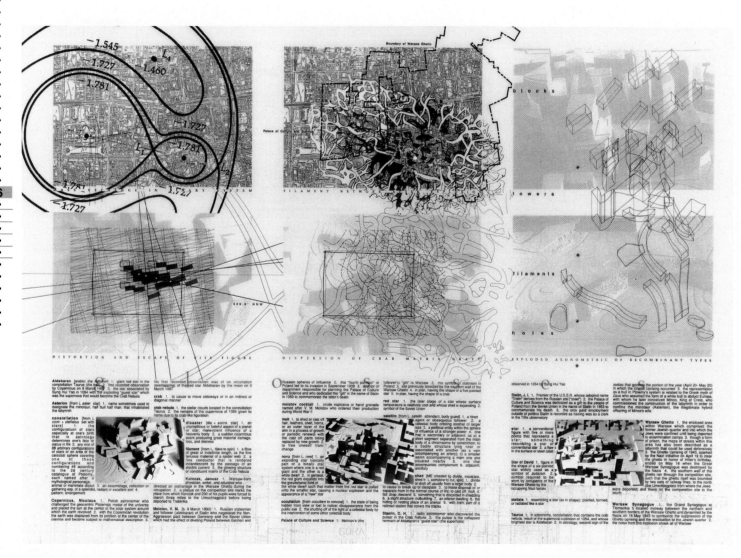

Drawing:

Competition board 1 of 3. Site diagrams, axonometric, model views and glossary entries arranged in a nine-square composition. An offset secondary and scaled nine-square begins in the second and third row of board 1 and continues as the program blocks on board 2. Projections beyond bounded areas integrate the elements and dissolve the purity of the nine square. Wash off halftone mylar, black ink line drawing, photocopy on adhesive film, transfer lettering, pressure-sensitive tape, photographs. 100cm x 70cm.

Design:

In contrast to either the easy identification or dialectical opposition of form and content, this project for the Warsaw city core pursues a diagrammatic approach and intensive use of information which at once maintains and subverts formal geometries and semiotic collages. The project suggests the complicity of politics, astronomy, religion, and the history of occupation through tropes of giant red stars, white dwarves, and the crab nebula.

166

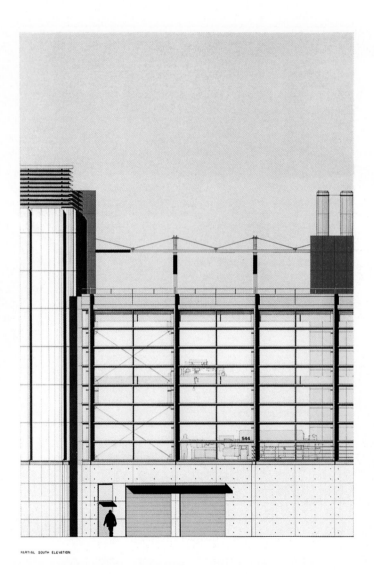

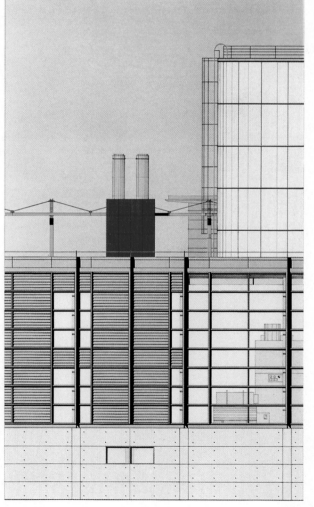

PARTIAL SOUTH ELEVATION

PARTIAL NORTH ELEVATION

Drawing:
Partial south and north elevation. KC-5 photographic reproduction with pantone on 36"x48" mylar.

Design:
Replacing an outmoded and environmentally unsound waste treatment plant, this facility will be constructed over a ten-year period and will remain fully operational throughout the process. Perimeter walls, bridges, towers, major axes, level changes, and color are used as ordering devices for all buildings and connections between them. Large areas of glass provide natural light in machinery rooms and by displaying the process, demystify it.

167

Alexis Pontvik Arkitekt, Stockholm, Sweden ━━━
Husarviken Urban Design Competition, Stockholm

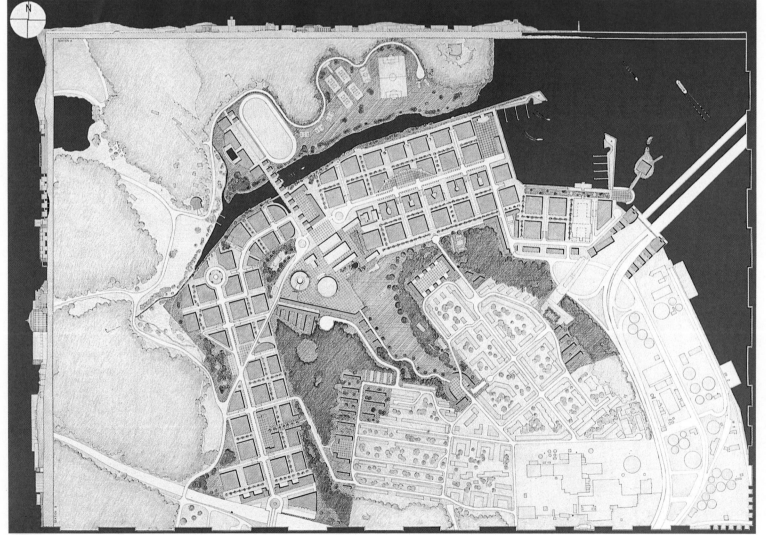

Drawing: ━━
Plan combined with sections. Ink on 594mm x 840mm polyester film. Copy colored with color pencil. The drawing shows the site plan of the competition area north of Stockholm. The proposed buildings are enhanced by thicker lines and hatching. In order to inform the onlooker two sections across the site have been placed at the edges. By showing the contours of landscape and building in conjunction with the plan the scale of the project can be deduced.

Design: ━━
Design based on an morphological analysis of some of the characteristics of the city of Stockholm, to which the site belongs. A regular pattern at first look, is in fact a series of local zones. The design refuses to extend beyond the water which is understood as a natural end to the expanding city.

5 **C**omposite • **P**rofessional **P**ortfolio

169

Drawing:

Watercolor and ink wash over pencil linework. Representative examples of 'outline' and 'compartition' (*finitio* and *partitio*) are treated as 'pages' from an imaginary text illustrating Leon Battista Alberti's writings on the art of building, superimposed over a plan and elevation of a new urban gateway for Beverly Hills, California.

Design:

This design for a gateway dedicated to Mnemosene (Memory, the mother of the muses), reiterates the architectural conventions found in the *Hortus Poeticus* nearly a mile distant. An urban iconography is thereby established, linking the two sites symbolically in a larger processional narrative.

Drawing: ━

Master plan. Night view. Ink on mylar, with zip-a-tone and airbrush color. 30" x 42".

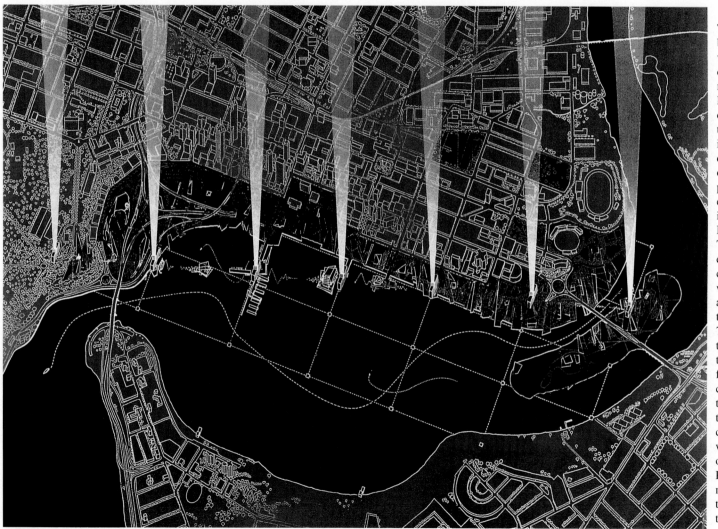

170

Design: ━

The concept of World Park is to bring Perth to the world and the world to Perth. The design process overlays traces of telecommunication waves along the landfilled area bounded by the city and Swan River. The registration of the resulting images is the organizational device that defines the landscape elements of the public park. The orbital path of Friendship 7 is delineated by a line of lights arrayed in an axial relationship from Mt. Eliza to Helrisson Island. The city grid was conceptually extended across the river, thus connecting the land and the water. Architectural elements are placed at the intersection of this extension and Friendship 7's orbital path. Coupled with the native Australian belief that the land is paper thin or merely floating on the water, this process allowed for the manipulation of the landscape through the removal or voiding of specific zones. Consequently, the water is exposed, and the nature of the landfill is revealed. World Park and Perth become a major node in a global communication network connected via electromagnetic waves.

Drawing:

Composite. Ink on mylar with zip-a-tone and model photograph.

Design:

The stackless library is an interactive center for electronic information access and retrieval, a cultural billboard promoting both technological browsing and research. The project questions the library's traditional building typology and formal resolution since it is no longer a repository of books, but a machine for information. Conceptually, stacks are unnecessary. Exploiting this allows for a resolution free from the constraints historically governed by the book physically.

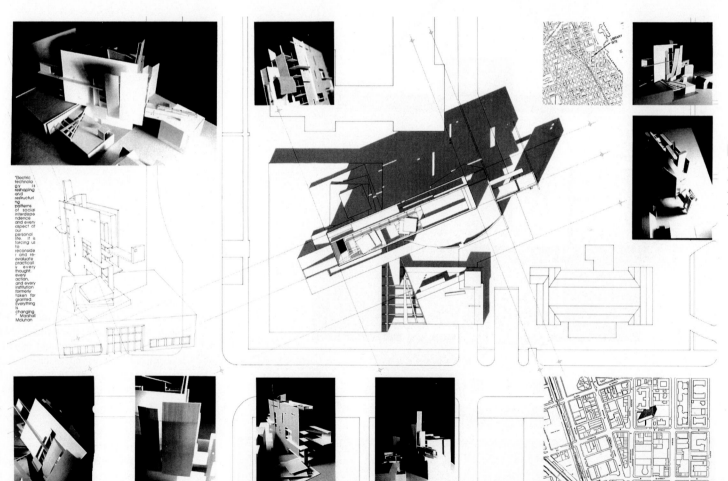

171

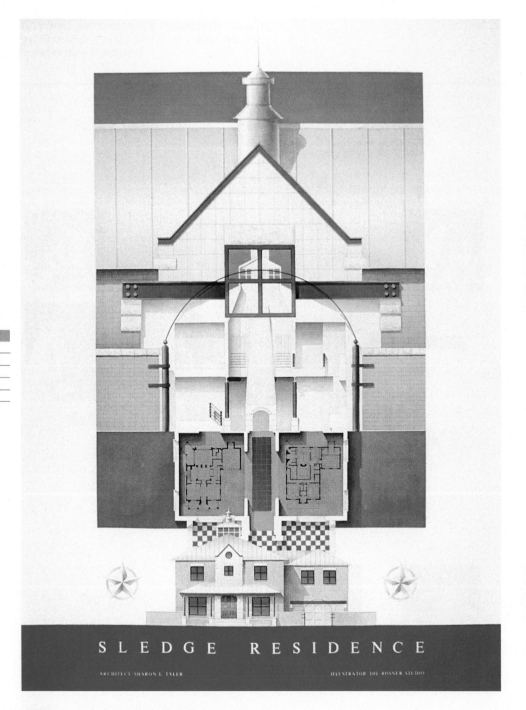

Joyce Rosner for Sharon I. Tyler Architect, Texas ▬
Sledge Residence, Houston, Texas

Drawing: ▬

Orthographic composite. Watercolor on Arches 140 lb. cold-press watercolor paper. This combination of orthographic views was inspired by a surrealistic collapsing of interior and exterior space. The use of plan and section illustrates the forms within, and the elements of varying scales define the structure and materiality of the space. Through a layering of images as well as the introduction of light source outside the drawing, a gravitational center is created, which radiates a sense of warmth thermally, visually, and graphically.

Design: ▬

The entry corridor axis which terminates at the fireplace, the hearth of the house, acts as a nucleus for the entire dwelling as well as for the underlying organization of the drawing. By revealing the relationship of this axis to the interior and exterior of the house, one understands the project through a simultaneous viewing of spaces.

Roth+Sheppard Architects, Colorado
Jeffrey L. Sheppard
Colorado House, S.W. Colorado Border

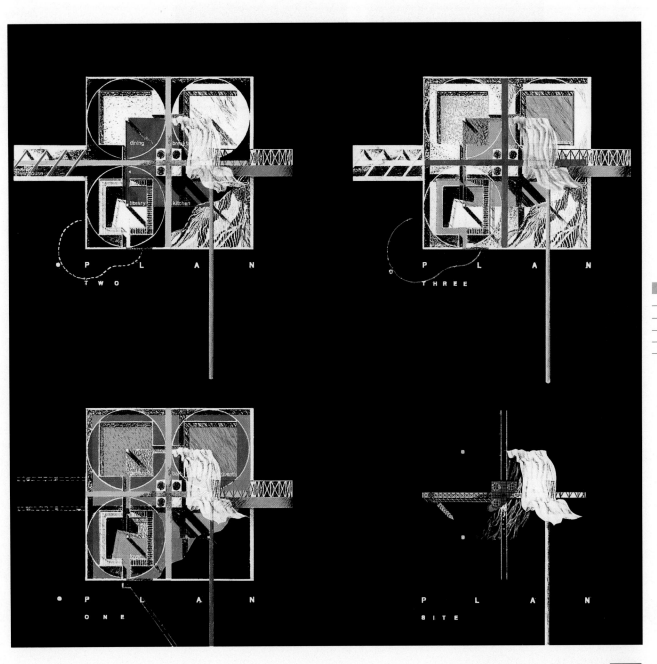

Drawing:

The second board of a two-board composition utilizing a collage of drawing media and printed material. Materials include black line prints, vinyl lettering, pen and ink, prismacolor, marker and white chalk on a black illustration board.

Design:

The juxtaposition of the mountains and plains collision forms the site of this winning entry in a regional design competition entitled 9 Houses. Agrarian imagery in both plan and section provide the patterns from which the design has evolved. Grided and eroded landscape, container elements, water towers and irrigated landscape are physically and metaphorically explored to formulate a variety of special, processional and enclosure experiences for the functional program of house. Note how the 4 square plan is explored in section, elevation, and within the center of the floor plan.

173

Roth+Sheppard Architects, Colorado
Jeffrey L. Sheppard
Arvada Apartments, Arvada, Colorado

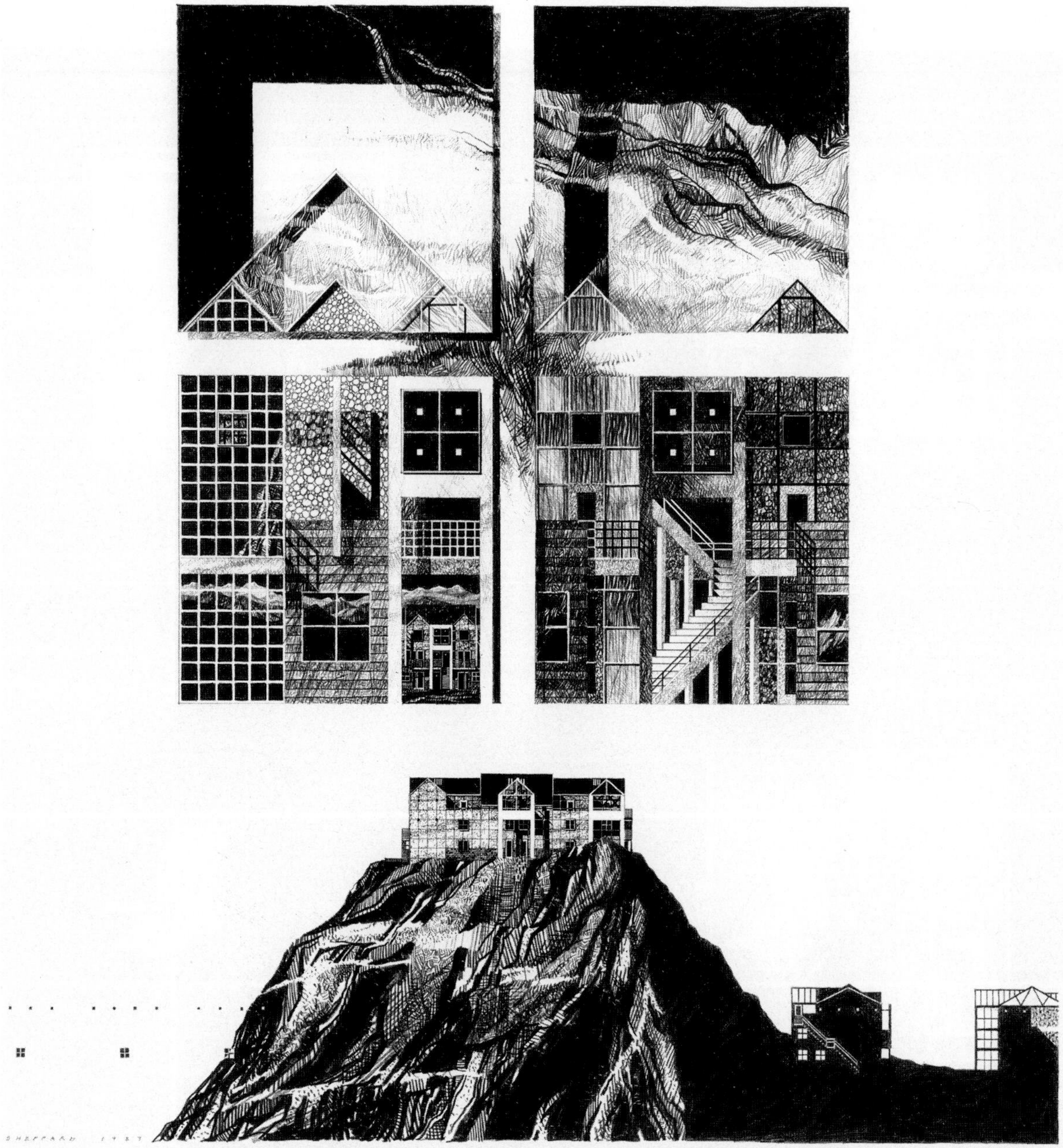

Drawing:

Plan, section and elevation overlay superimposing ten different scaled images of the various components of the project. Pen and ink, graphite, charcoal and prismacolor on 1000H paper. 24"x36".

Design:

This 11-unit, low-cost apartment complex utilizes a plan and elevation layering system to modulate the overall reading of the exterior. The grid and textural surface juxtapositions enhance the notion of townhouse, tenant identity, and coherent whole. Various window and massing treatments further explore the notion of single and double height space, scale and plan/facade relationship.

Joel Sanders, Architect, New York
Joel Sanders and Mark Tsurumaki
Kyle Residence: The House as Viewing Apparatus, Houston, Texas

Drawing:

"Constructed Landscape"-The Lawn-View from the Dining Area. Ink, pantone on mylar. 24"x36". This drawing is a composite plan/perspective, relating the observer's vantage point and cone of vision within the dining area with a corresponding view of the backyard. The lawn, the icon of suburban nature, becomes a folded surface that defines the skylit roof of the master bedroom below. Its upward incline raises the level of the horizon, replacing the view of neighbors with an alternative landscape--the lawn meeting the sky. A pivoting outdoor video screen--a virtual window--dematerializes the boundaries of the site.

Design:

This project rethinks a central tenet of modernism--"transparency"--the dissolution of the boundary separating the inside from the outside world according to the requirements of contemporary suburban life. A utility core is extruded from the house and becomes a wall which follows the property line and encloses the site. Viewed from outside the bounding wall creates visual privacy, shielding the house from neighbors. Viewed from within, the wall is dematerialized; the glass walls of the house frame views of a constructed landscape, produced not by nature but by culture--the media and the architect.

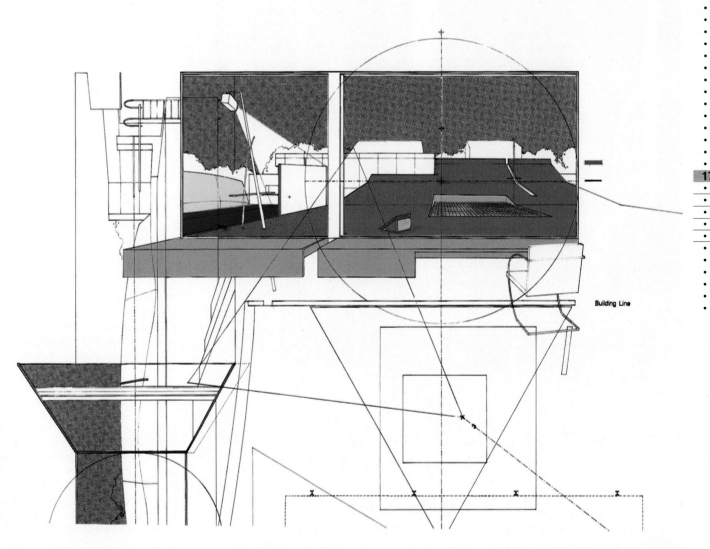

Building Line

The historic TIMES TOWER, with its structural grid clad in stainless steel, pulsating with laser beams from the TIMES CENTER towers, festooned with great illuminated signs, locates the heart of THE GREAT WHITE WAY. The world's most powerful beacon lances into the night sky. THE CROSSROADS OF THE WORLD is a phantasmagoria of light and movement. The new TIMES SQUARE is like the old one, simply more so.

CITY LIGHTS
THE TIMES TOWER ON THE GREAT WHITE WAY

176

Frederic Schwartz, New York
City Lights: Times Square Competition, New York, New York, 1984

Drawing:

This original night-time perspective is a composite technique combining a drawing by hand over a photograph of the existing context and by use of traditional perspective methods to construct the new design. A #2 MONGOL pencil on mylar was used to make the drawing. A KC-5 photographic high contrast print was made from the original and colored with Panatone film overlay.

Design:

Even though this project "lost," the ideas of this submission are now being employed by the authorities involved with the redevelopment of the site. The lighting solution consists of four lighting components. The world's most powerful light beacon shooting straight up from the framework of the tower; the return of the old *New York Times* electronic news sign; giant rear-view projected signs and computerized message units sold to finance the project and rented to pay for the electric bill and a web of dancing computerized lasers emitting from the architrave of the new towers.

Drawings:

Drawings for Buckhead Branch Library are ink on mylar, produced by hand with a pin-bar system of overlays. Poché, notes, discrete layers of information are drawn on separate sheets and combined photographically.

Design:

The existing "Ida Williams Branch" is a parking meter... past expired... unable to communicate with speed and clarity. The function of today's public library; a locus for knowledge within a civic landscape bounded by mobile sprawl and strip shopping. The particular site is atop a crest that commands a spectacular view of downtown Atlanta. The new building consumes the large narrow portion of the site in-between the distinct frontages while perching itself in full view toward downtown. An array of canopies intensifies the pedestrian scale relationships along Buckhead Avenue and deposits the reader at the helm of the spectator city, air-conditioned and detached. The plan organization is linear: sidewalk, entry sequence, circulation desk, reference and main reading room. Additional functions: children's services, public meeting room and periodicals are located in "saddle bags" off the main linear circulation path.

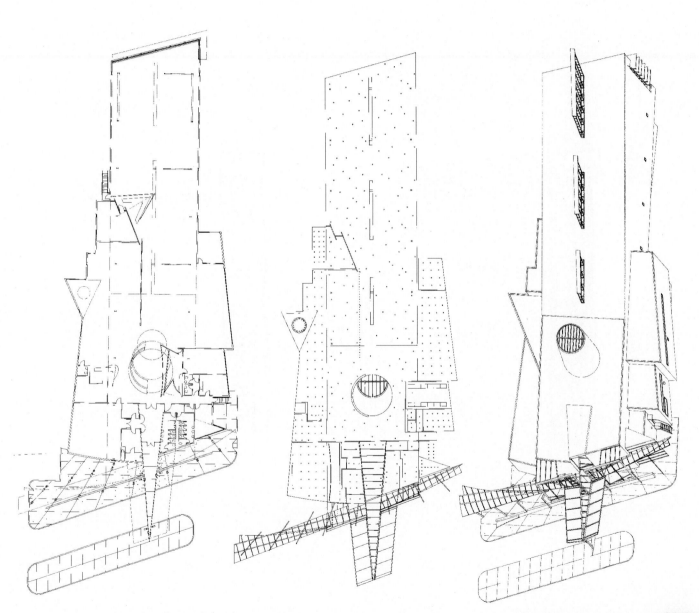

177

178

Drawings: ▬

Drawing on the left is a computer drawing that describes geometrically the gentle curves of the house and their spheres of influence into the woods. The plan was eventually dimensioned from a longitudinal "center" line with perpendiculars at each sixty-fourth of an inch using computer-generated mathematics. Drawing on the right is a composite ink on mylar, hand drawn on a pin-bar system and photographically combined.

Design: ▬

Where the tree had fallen, an opening occurred in the woods. The house occupies the position of the fallen tree. The house also occupies the attitude of the people who inhabit it; an attitude of multiplicities and dualities. The house is firmly planted on the ground but rises above it. The interior spaces enclose and protect and, at the same time, imply extensions into the space of the woods. Particular exterior zones are one with particular interior zones. The house is narrow but not limited. It is isolated in the woods yet at its very heart is the goshinden room where light and companionship are shared.

Kevin D. Scott, Colorado
Architect's Trap (the board game)

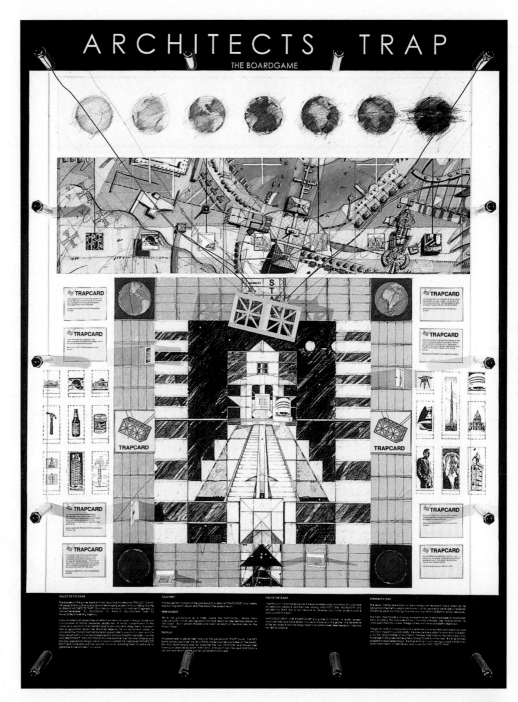

Drawing:

The "Architect's Trap" is a three-dimensional construction of paper, graphite, prismacolor, xerox, high contrast photo images, basswood, wire, steel framing rods, and plexiglass.

Design:

Through the use and play of an actual boardgame and visual metaphors the "Architect's Trap" is a didactic source to "awaken" us all to the necessity of environmentally correct architectural development.

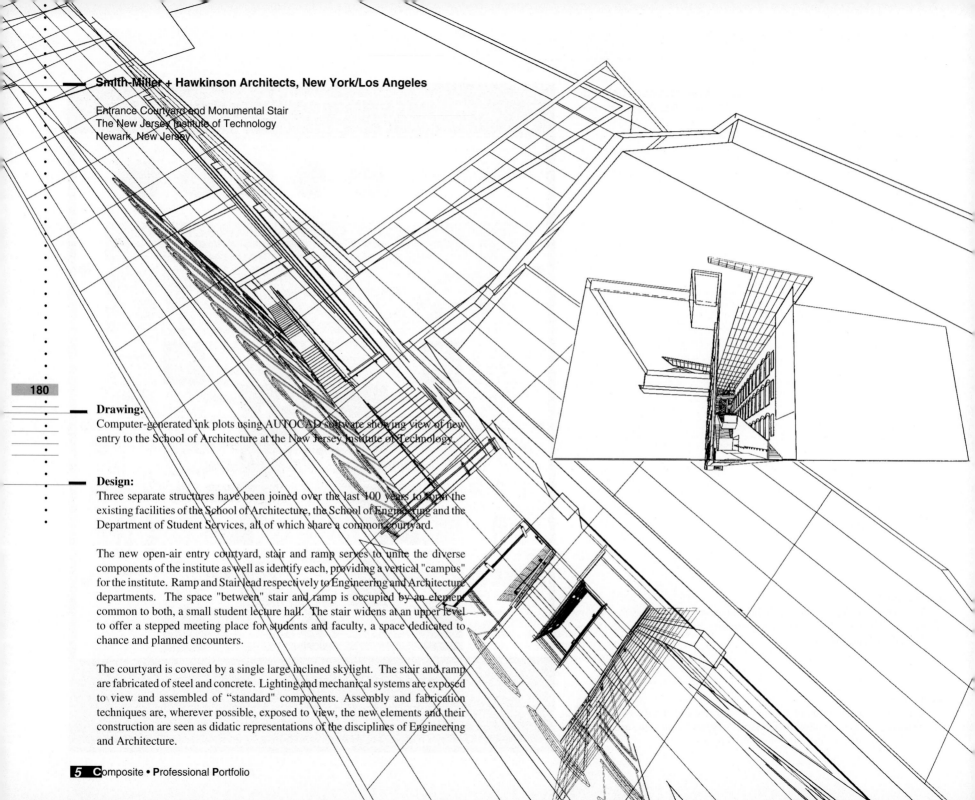

Smith-Miller + Hawkinson Architects, New York/Los Angeles

Entrance Courtyard and Monumental Stair
The New Jersey Institute of Technology
Newark, New Jersey

Drawing:
Computer-generated ink plots using AUTOCAD software showing view of new entry to the School of Architecture at the New Jersey Institute of Technology.

Design:
Three separate structures have been joined over the last 100 years to form the existing facilities of the School of Architecture, the School of Engineering and the Department of Student Services, all of which share a common courtyard.

The new open-air entry courtyard, stair and ramp serves to unite the diverse components of the institute as well as identify each, providing a vertical "campus" for the institute. Ramp and Stair lead respectively to Engineering and Architecture departments. The space "between" stair and ramp is occupied by an element common to both, a small student lecture hall. The stair widens at an upper level to offer a stepped meeting place for students and faculty, a space dedicated to chance and planned encounters.

The courtyard is covered by a single large inclined skylight. The stair and ramp are fabricated of steel and concrete. Lighting and mechanical systems are exposed to view and assembled of "standard" components. Assembly and fabrication techniques are, wherever possible, exposed to view, the new elements and their construction are seen as didatic representations of the disciplines of Engineering and Architecture.

Smith-Miller + Hawkinson Architects, New York/Los Angeles

"Imperfect Utopia: A Park for the New World"
Phase 1, "The Textualized Landscape"
Amphitheater and Outdoor Cinema
North Carolina Museum of Art, Raleigh, North Carolina

In collaboration with:
Barbara Kruger, Artist
Nicholas Quennell, Quennell Rothschild Landscape Architects
Creative Inc., 3D Animation

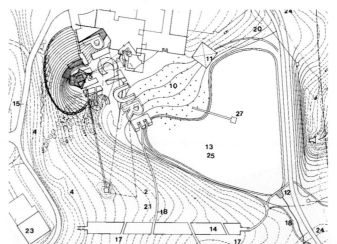

Drawing:

Ink on mylar plan of *The Textualized Landscape* (top right). Frame number 002745 of a 3D Studio animation walkthrough generated from AUTOCAD construction documents. Transparent perspective from below amphitheater looking at projection booth and cinema beyond (bottom right).

Design:

The Textualized Landscape, the first phase of "Imperfect Utopia: A Park for the New World" melds the notions of *SPECTACLE, SITE,* and *TEXT* into an inclusive kind of public space which expands the museum's capacity for outdoor programs. Engaging ideas of *HISTORY, CULTURE, GEOGRAPHY,* and *TOPOGRAPHY,* this *PUBLIC SPACE* provides an accessible place for a variety of experiences in the landscape.

The site of the amphitheater and outdoor cinema is located close to the museum, and provides the first opportunity to interpret some of the ideas of the larger plan previously developed by this team of architects, artist and landscape architect.

The project may be seen as being comprised of a series of sculptural elements, spaces and experiences that also functions programmatically as stage, screen, and seating for a variety of museum events.

181

Thomas Sofranko, Assistant Professor ▬
Louisiana State University, Baton Rouge, Louisiana
Spirit House 4

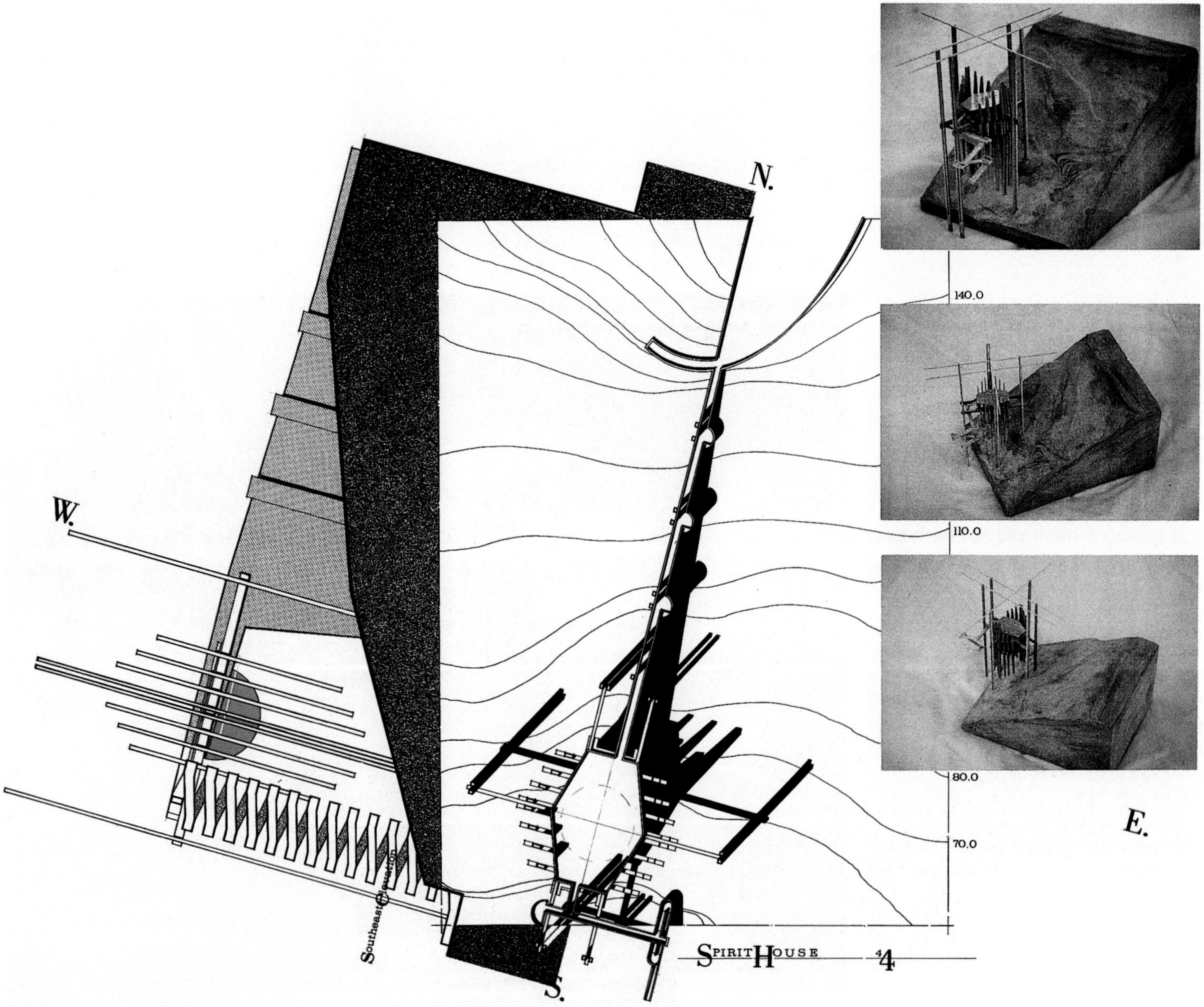

N.

140.0

110.0

80.0

70.0

W.

E.

Southeast Elevation

SPIRIT HOUSE 4

Drawing: ▬

Ink on vellum, film
and photographs.
Overlay of drawings
with a central focus
on the plan/section
relationship. Photo-
graphs become an
animated sequence of
circling from above.

Design: ▬

The Spirit Houses are
an ongoing series
which investigates
various ideas of or-
der, site and domes-
ticity. Spirit House 4
considers the creation
of a personal space
through separation.

Shin Takamatsu Architect & Associates, Japan
Syntax, Sakyo-ku, Kyoto, Japan

Drawing:

Compositional section. Black-and-white airbrush drawing on laminated tracing paper. An ambiguously illuminated building, set against a dark sky, appears an object without context. Variously elaborated independent elements of different scales, materials, textures and degrees of details are carefully composed with dark and deep shadows to create a strong unified whole.

Design:

This is an avant-garde building which is conspicuously striking even on Kitayama Street, which is said to be the cutting-edge fashion street in Kyoto. The building's external appearance itself is a sign. The aim of its design was a search for what "power" should be. The building is a small sea filled with a flotilla of independent elements. It is a sea with no charts to navigate it by. Here there is adventure, discovery and also some danger.

Minoru Takeyama, Japan

Tokyo International Port Terminal, Tokyo, Japan

Drawing:

Axonometrics. Pencil on illustration board. Ink for paving pattern. The upper drawing indicates the vertical orchestration of the different spaces which compose the port terminal building. The three lower floors are closely related by the open terraces, decks, stairs, open corridor with similar floor patterns. The lower drawing shows floor patterns of these public spaces.

Design:

The port terminal is primarily for international passenger boats. The site is on a reclaimed island located close to the center of the city and in the waterfront park. The form of "houseness" was conceived by creating a manmade hill, or multiple terraces of platforms, which covers the main body and cascades down to the street level. This is intended to be landmark and seamark which is simple, dominant, and identical from all directions. Visual interests are created (depending upon the viewing distance) by the solid-void of internal forms and external framework, scale, surface treatment, color, and light and shade.

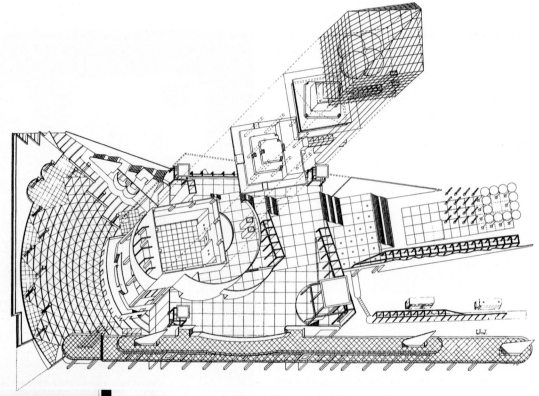

Christine Tedesco, Adjunct Professor
Charles E. Daniel Center for Building Research, Genoa, Italy
"Aqueducts, Cisterns and the Tarantella"

Drawing:

Composite drawing No. 1A/aggregate information, reversed positive ink on mylar transfer. Composite image contains selected elements drawn from the entire set of basic information (pipe sections of aqueduct system, fragments of elevation, plan, and section of aqueduct and stair, etc.).

Design:

This drawing (part of the total set) is a result of an investigation that led to study the Tarantella, a southern Italian folk dance for women, and a parallel survey of the medieval aqueduct system in the city of Genoa, Italy. This drawing marks the first in a series of generative composite drawings that attempt to transfer and transform the basic information gathered in the previous overlay drawing series.

185

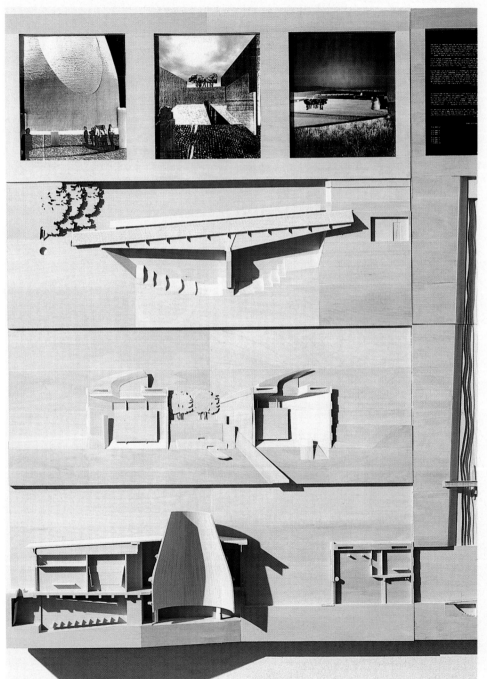

Tod Williams Billie Tsien and Associates, New York ▬
Los Angeles Arts Park

Drawing: ▬

Collage and wood drawing. Combination of model-making technique and drawing. This panel, one of three, shows three traditional collages on top. These were created from color photocopies of photographs and show: 1) the Entry Court, 2) Interior Courtyard, and 3) Sculpture Pavilion. The three wood drawings are done within a depth of 1". Relief drawings in basswood show: 1) Bridge in axonometric, 2) section through the Museum in perspective, and 3) Sculpture Pavilion as a section.

Design:

The winning entry in an International Design Competition for the Los Angeles Arts Park, is a Museum and Cultural Center for the San Fernando Valley. It consists of a Gateway Building housing two Galleries, housing for Artists in Residence, and an Outdoor Sculpture Area attached by a bridge. Project done in collaboration with the sculptor Elyn Zimmerman and landscape architect Cheryl Barton.

Drawing:

Plan. Computer-generated night simulation.

Design:

Eight-thousand square meters of an international center for the contemporary arts (a school, a film studio, a *mediathe`que*, spectacle and exhibition halls, two cinemas, laboratories for research and production, administrative offices, housing and a bar/ restaurant) inserted into existing Le Fresnoy, built in the twenties. Conceptually the project was interpreted as a succession of boxes inside a box. Under the large electronic roof are the boxes of the existing building, most hereafter sheltered from the bad weather. The new facilities located in the existing volumes conceived as technically autonomous boxes while maintaining the fluidity of the Fresnoy spaces. At Fresnoy the design intent speaks of an "architecture-event" rather than an "architecture-object." The interstitial space between the new and old roofs becomes a place of fantasies and experiments (filming and other exploratory works on space and time). The "in-between" becomes a condenser of interdisciplinary investigations between teaching and research, art and cinema, music and image.

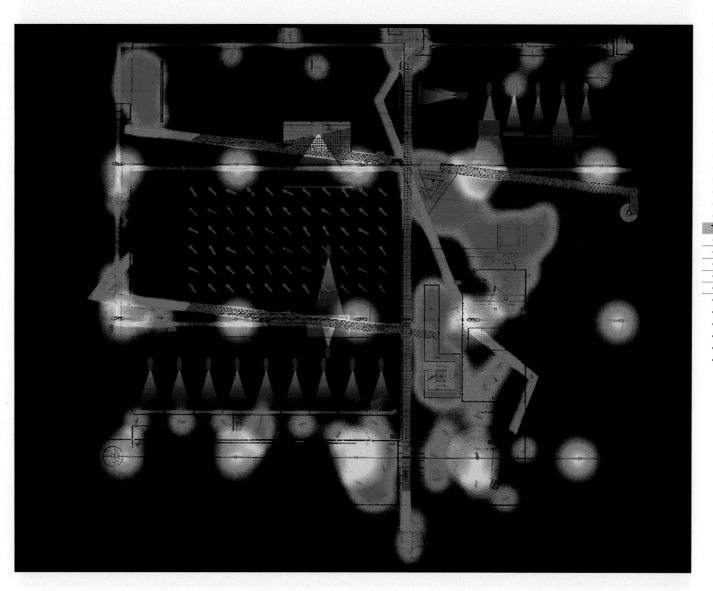

187

188

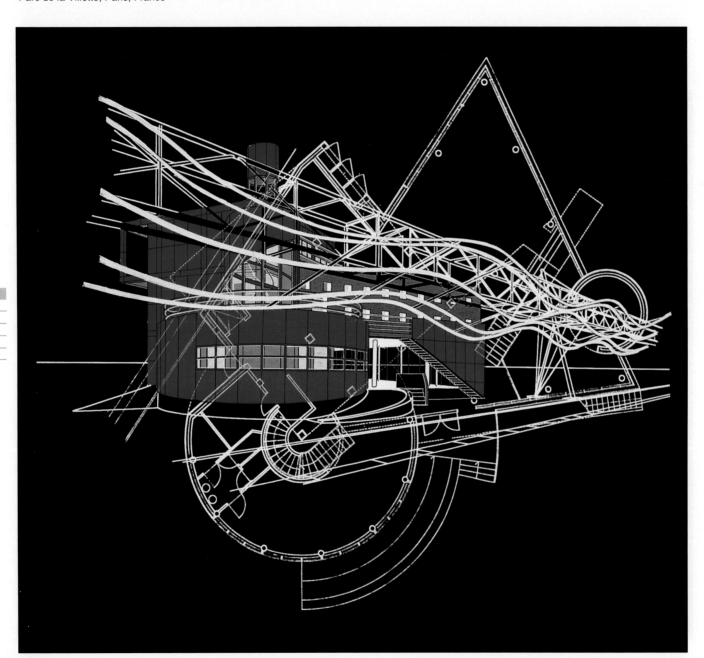

Drawing:
Plan and perspective superimposed (Folie L3). Ink and acrylic on paper.

Design:
Over one kilometer long in one direction and seven-hundred meters in the other, the park as designated in the competition was to be no simple landscape replica. On the contrary, the brief for this "Urban Park for the 21st Century" develops a complex program of cultural and entertainment facilities encompassing open air theaters, restaurants, art galleries, music and painting workshops, playgrounds, video and computer displays, as well as the obligatory gardens where cultural invention rather than natural re-creation, were encouraged. This winning design scheme had been conceived as a large metropolitan venture, derived from the disjunctions and dissociations of our time. It attempted to propose a new urbanistic strategy by articulating concepts such as "superimposition," architectural "combination" and "cinematic" landscapes. Tschumi described the park as "the largest discontinuous building in the world."

M. Saleh Uddin, Associate Professor
Southern University, Baton Rouge, Louisiana
Rahman Residence, Dhaka, Bangladesh

Drawing:
Photocollage using presentation plans and a 3D drawing, construction plans, and photographs of the completed front facade and interior stair details. Photographs superimposed on drawings copied on color pantone film and negative prints.

Design:
One family residence with the provision of vertical expansion without sacrificing the privacy of the current design. Restricted site boundaries forced the design to be sculpted from a cubic mass-volume. Subtracted mass in the front protects the glazed wall, and sucks air inside the building which counterbalances the double-height void in the dining area, facilitating natural air-flow year-round. All openings were carefully designed (most openings pushed inward to avoid direct confrontation with climatic extremes) to respond to the environmental conditions of the region's hot, humid climate.

189

190

Drawing:
Compositional section-elevation. Airbrush and color ink on white Kent paper. 1150mm x 670mm.

Design:

Hamlet is a multi-unit housing for four households, representing the grandparents and the families of their two sons and one daughter with children, all living under one huge translucent tent made of Teflon membrane. The households are all independently situated but share small spaces together for common living which creates a curious balance between an apartment building and a single house constructed for one large family. Above the concrete of the ground floor rises the steel structure which combines with the membrane to create privacy against the surrounding.

Riken Yamamoto + Field Shop, Yokohama, Japan
Gazebo, Yokohama, Japan

Drawing:
Compositional elevation. Airbrush and color ink on white Kent paper. 640mm x 890mm.

Design:
Gazebo is an urban building for complex use, containing shops in the ground floor, office and apartments in the upper floors with the owners' housing on top. The main reinforced concrete structure is partly covered by suspended steel mesh which organizes the elevation against the street. A freestanding roof covers most of the different outdoor spaces which are interacting with the housing part on top of the building.

192

Drawing:
Rotated perspective with clothing patterns superimposed. Ink on mylar and acrylic paint.

■ Mehrdad Yazdani, California
Overland House, Los Angeles, California

■ Drawings: Study sketches. Pencil on trace paper.
Perspective and site plan composite. Pencil on mylar.

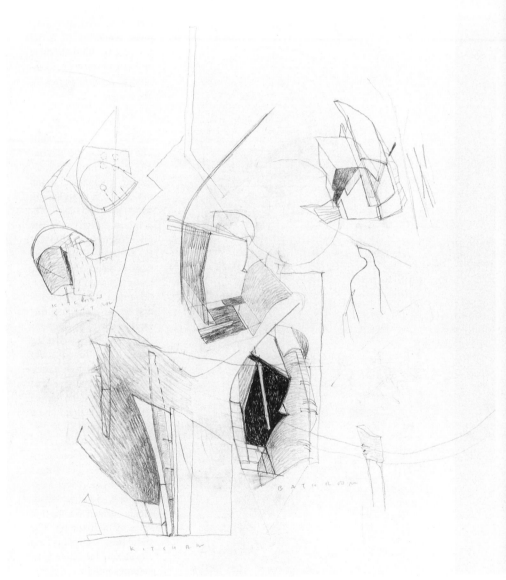

Ken Yeang, Selangor, Malaysia
China Tower #3, Haikou, China

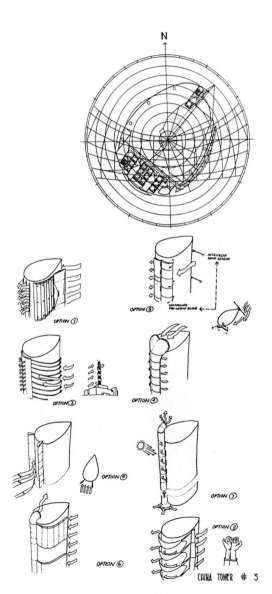

Drawings:
Study sketches of wind collection devices, and computer rendering of aerial perspective. 3D model done on Fastcad software. *Computer drawing by Derick Ng See Leng.*

Design:
The site lies in the hot, humid island climatic belt allowing the architect to tap into the site's prevailing wind conditions as a predominant design factor. The tower itself has an elliptical floor-plate oriented at its narrowest end to receive the incoming wind. A composite number of wind-collection devices are adopted that include devices such as 'wind-catcher' fins over the entire length of the south facade to accelerate, direct, and channel the wind into the building. At the top is a revolving restaurant and a large wind-scoop that collects, stores and provides partial ambient wind-energy for the building's emergency electrical back-up supply. Solar sun-shading is located on the hot sides of the building. The staircases, restrooms and elevator lobbies all receive natural sunlight.

Drawings:

Plan and elevation. Airbrush on ink line drawings on 12"x 12" rice paper.

Design:

'Metonymic-Oku' Linear Light Fixture. The intention of this in progress investigation was to further expand earlier studies on the concept of Japanese inner space and envelopment which emphasizes horizontality and seeks symbolic and spiritual depths. The investigation involves the application of the 'oku' theory to the nature of a human form to further question its validity. It embraces the knowledge graphology, chiromancy, chirognamy, geomacy and astrology as a process of enveloping an inner space. These geometric forms become a set of overlapping transparent layers allowing a penetration of perceptions within the depthless space. Through this process the inner space is contracted into a narrow vertical slit.

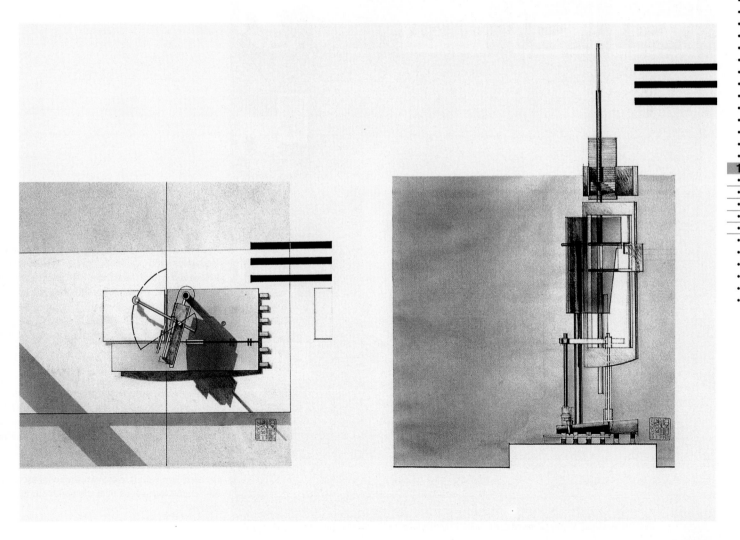

195

Art Zendarski for Ellerbe Becket, Kansas City ▬

New Boston Gardens, Boston, Massachusetts

Drawing: ▬

Perspective and plan composite. Black pencil with oils on paper. 15"x24". The bird's-eye view rendering of the proposed arena was drawn in black pencil. Reductions and exploded details of the pencil rendering were used to emphasize key architectural elements. The drawing details along with the computer-generated plan of the arena were then silkscreened onto a drawing board. Color was applied with oil stains. The intent of the composite drawing technique was to communicate the complex arena concept to the general public without sacrificing the dynamic spirit and energy of the design.

Design: ▬

As the anchor component to one of the nation's most prestigious mixed-use developments, the New Boston Gardens will be the strategic entrance to Boston from the north shore. The complex will literally function as a machine for processing thousands of people daily for a variety of entertainment opportunities. Due to its high visibility from the future adjacent highrise towers, the roof is seen as a fifth elevation. Designed as a "starched white handkerchief" laid over the trusses, it is shifted out of orthogonal to create a sense of movement. Exposed and expressed mechanical elements emphasize the machine aesthetic of the design.

Drawing:

Site plan and perspective sketch. Ink on mylar with color film (site plan). Pentel pen on Strathmore sketch paper (perspective).

Design:

Fellowship Statement of Purpose: "We seek to provide an atmosphere of warm companionship for free and inquiring minds, searching together for finer religious, ethical and social truths." . . . Because their values are humanistic rather than theistic and their budget modest, the fellowship requested that this facility have a distinctly human scale and use 'honest' materials simply and creatively.

197

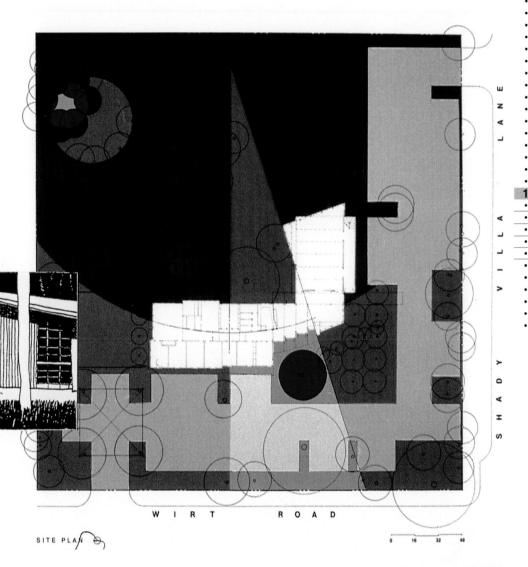

SITE PLAN

0   16   32   48